This book is a chronicle and testimony for our capacity to enter into the pain of being human, without resistance, and emerge, again and again, into a state of nondual awareness. The extremes of heartbreak and profound spiritual awakening couldn't be rendered more starkly, yet they are so close. Though the path of *being broken wide open* begins in our pain and anguish, like all true paths, it leads to the state of embodied transcendence. That the heart can turn so quickly? This is the real miracle. Rashani's poem is a wonder. In the space of just a few words, she takes our soul in her hands and shows how we can move from the depths of despair to a place of immutable wholeness.

—**Peter Fenner**, author of *Radiant Mind* and *The Edge of Certainty*

In clarity, precision, honesty, and strength, which are rooted in the infinite, Rashani illustrates the twilight zone of the experience of knowing our true nature. In a milieu where even spiritual writers are influenced by the Hollywood happy ending—in their domain, it's called enlightenment—Rashani presents a clear, gemmed, and fiercely independent voice. Rashani writes about the whole spectrum of states that make up the human experience. She also embraces our experience of fragile moments and courageously reaches into the deepest pain ingrained in them; she transforms dualism, both the beauty and the ugly, into oneness of being.

—**Smadar De Lange**

This is a book from the deep that finds light not by seeking light, but by letting go into darkness. It is a book of miracles—not the usual kind of miracles like walking on water—but the miracle of finding beauty and love and transcendence in the very heart of life with all its brokenness and loss. It's a poem, really, or a song or a sutra. I love the way Rashani weaves together the beautiful and the ugly so that we can see how inseparable they are and how she conveys so much so sparingly. This book is a beautiful, powerful, gorgeous song of life and death.

—**Joan Tollifson,** author of *Bare-Bones Meditation: Waking Up from the Story of My Life*

Medicine comes in as many forms as our prodigious planet offers, but why do we feel surprised when its form is suffering? This is the old, moonlit path itself. Awakening cannot be separate from suffering; resurrection cannot be other than the full embrace of loss. *Beyond Brokenness* is the potent medicine of grief turned to praise. It sanctions us all to dare to be fully human and to take up the song! That's what we're here for.

—**Susan Murphy**, roshi. Author of *Upside Down Zen*

As the heart awakens and the palette of experience expands, we can find ourselves pioneers of subtle inner landscapes. At times the unfolding vistas are beautiful and awe inspiring, at others unsettling, painful, and even scary. Rashani Réa has courageously journeyed forth into the terrain of the soul and returned with a bejeweled heart of wisdom. This eloquent and deeply personal account of her life and the genesis of "The Unbroken" is a gift and resource to all aspirants of Truth. For anyone passing through a threshold of uncertainty or pain, *Beyond Brokenness* helps provide the insight and support needed to allow life to unfold and reveal our soul's next vista.

—**Taj Inayat**

Rashani's inspired poem has such an impact because it points to depths that we need to find and connect with. The letters interweave beautifully with her poem and story, helping us become aware that we are not alone either in our suffering or in our healing, and that our shared journey toward oneness furthers a greater transformation that we all need here on earth.

—**Judith Saly**, pathwork teacher

Rarely do we get the gift, not only of a poem that raises up the soul, but also the story of the poem and the story of the poet. Rashani's own suffering and personal pain reunite us with parts of ourselves we try to deny. I'm thankful to have received so many insights in this meaningful book.

—**James Fadiman,** Ph.D. co-editor of *Essential Sufism*, author of *The Other Side of Haight*

When her deepest knowing brings pain, Rashani willingly walks through the flames until what remains is pure essence of truth.

—**Cassandra Wylie**, MSW, therapist

Rashani tenderly inspires us towards compassion with the entirety of ourselves, both for our known suffering and the surprising passion that exists within the wholeness of our infinite lives.

—**Lynton Dove White**, author of *Canoe Plants of Ancient Hawai'i*

This is the deep, intimate narrative of a journey that by its singularity speaks to us all. I have known Rashani as a singer and songwriter of powerfully evocative songs and am delighted now to discover that same unique voice rising up from the printed page.

—**Caitriona Reed**, Zen teacher and founder of Manzanita Village Retreat

Also by the author

The Unfurling of an Artist
My Bird Has Come Home
Tao and the Moon
In Praise of Love
Welcome to the Feast
It's Time For a Miracle
Soetry: Songs and Poetry
The Way Moonlight Touches
Is The Bowl Empty or Is It Filled with Moonlight?

Beyond Brokenness

Rashani Réa

Foreword by Mirabai Starr
Introduction to "The Unbroken"
by Tom Joyce

Copyright © 2009 by Rashani Réa.

Library of Congress Control Number: 2008908674
ISBN: Hardcover   978-1-4363-7293-0
              Softcover   978-1-4363-7292-3

All rights reserved. No part of this book may be reproduced or transmitted in any form or by any means, electronic or mechanical, including photocopying, recording, or by any information storage and retrieval system, without permission in writing from the copyright owner.

This book was printed in the United States of America.

To order additional copies of this book, contact:

Xlibris Corporation

1-888-795-4274

www.Xlibris.com

Orders@Xlibris.com

53446

Contents

Acknowledgments 19
Foreword 27

Part I
Childhood 35
Another Perspective 91
France 103
Grieving 123
Talons Of The Dawn 139

Part II
The Unbroken 163
The Poem 169
Worship 185
Endarkenment 197
The Poem's Journey 215
Joanna 221
Selected Letters 233

Afterword 255

Appendices
Appendix A 267
Appendix B 269
Appendix C 270
Appendix D 272
Appendix E 273
Appendix F 274

Index 277

Collages

Eons old, 1988 15
Love births quietly, 1990 39
Let it be nameless, 1999 51
We are made gentle by love, 1992 81
Love isn't something we do, 2001 97
Two ferns, 1990 121
Two ferns, 1990 135
Is the bowl empty or is it filled
with moonlight? 2003 195
Prayerflag and bodhi leaf, 2003 205
Where I thought I'd find, 2001 211
Beyond Brokenness, 2008 231
Recent collage of *The Unbroken*, 2008 283

To my parents
My brothers, Charlie and Bruce
To Tao, my son
To Ma Anandamayi
Diane, Doathéa, and Joseph
Malia, Martin, Shanti Giovanna
Moritz, Margaret, Ian, and Ann
To my extended family
too numerous to name
and to the unknowable essence
that remains *unbroken*
amidst the many breakings
in a given lifetime

Reality is not as it seems. Nor is it different.

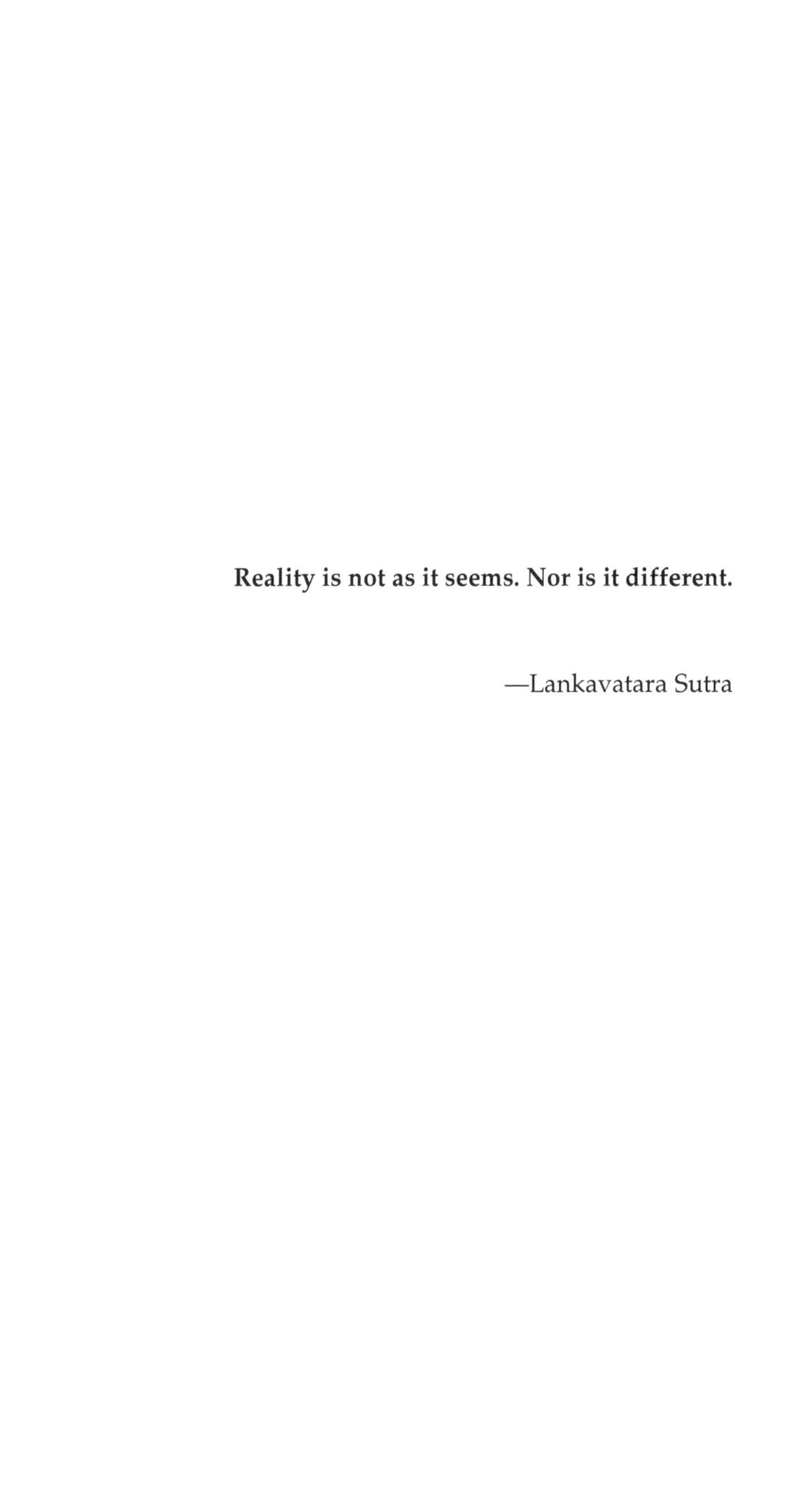

—Lankavatara Sutra

Beyond Brokenness

The story of a poem,
"The Unbroken,"
written by Rashani Réa in 1991.

Its genesis, afterthoughts
and a few of many responses.

Acknowledgments

This book has been gestating for many years. I can't honestly say *when* it was begun. It feels as if it were writing itself silently before I had any intention of writing a book and intermittently showing up in my dreams. Then, several friends in different places began encouraging me to write. A seed was planted, and I remember speaking about *the book* for years. I offer thanks to my friends who are scattered constellations on every continent and have stayed in touch through decades of geographical separation. Each of you is woven into these pages.

Just when I was planning to sit down and finally write *the book*, life guided me in an unexpected direction. I was taken to an indigenous forest bordering an abandoned field strewn with fallen ancient stonewalls a few miles from my home in Hawai'i. Nearing fifty, I had spent the previous twenty-eight years creating sanctuaries, planting trees, living in community, and was soon, or so I thought, to put down the hammer and nails, pickax, and saw. I was secretly dreaming of a small simple open cottage with a view of the ocean, far from any signs of civilization and definitely *not* in a community. A friend told me, "When you turn fifty, you will enter into the state of jubilation." At the time, jubilation to me sounded, looked, felt, and smelled like solitude and silence. Through a series of synchronistic events, I became the steward of this 'aina,[1] and a local elder assured me that *jubilation* would be nothing that I could possibly imagine and, more than likely, the opposite of what I thought.

Sure enough.

My mind was perplexed, as were most of my friends that I chose to leave behind a beautiful well-established retreat center that I had spent twelve years creating for

---

[1] The Hawaiian word for *land*, which means, "that which nourishes and feeds us."

an overgrown tangle of wild weeds in a forest and a windswept field of collapsing walls. Had I lost my mind? For the first two years, I rebuilt fallen walls, one rock at a time, cleared large areas of ginny grass with WWOOFers,[2] friends, and retreatants who joined me for monthlong intensives throughout the year and began planting native Hawaiian trees and bountiful gardens. I designed and built an octagonal home overlooking the ocean and several simple structures for retreatants and guests. Now, five years later, with the help of nearly two hundred dedicated helpers, I have co-created another sanctuary. It was given its name, Kipukamaluhialaʻakea[3] by a Hawaiian kahuna.

My motto, "One rock at a time" or "One nail at a time," depending on the project, allowed me to stay in the moment without becoming overwhelmed by such an enormous undertaking. I give boundless thanks to the many devoted people who believed in this vision; without whom, it would not exist as it does today.

---

[2] Willing workers on organic farms.
[3] *Kipuka*: Variation or change of form, as an opening in a forest; an oasis or island, often vegetated; of older land surrounded by a more recent lava flow. *Maluhia*: Peace, quiet, security, restful, serenity, awe and stillness that reigned during some of the ancient ceremonies: peaceful. To cause or give peace; protect: A place of worship. *Laʻakea*: Sacred light. (*Kipukamaluhia* for short!)

How does one thank the 'aina, the spirit of the land, except by caring for it over time? The years of loving and caring for Kipukamaluhia, many hours a day, prepared me for writing this book. This indescribable 'aina, more than any teacher or teaching, invites me back to the moment again and again, humbles me into silence many times a day, and brings me back to the immediacy of what is. With inestimable gratitude, I offer thanks to the ancestors of this land whose presence I am aware of often, to the earth in whose richness my hands find deep healing and from whose abundance my entire being has remembered the naturalness and jubilation of *simply this*.

This sanctuary is my *real* book, a three-dimensional, edible collage with no words. *Beyond Brokenness* is a small aperture into my life, more a mandala or medicine wheel than a book, though it is written in straight lines on pages that *look* like a book. It would be impossible to list every being and ecosystem that has been a part of the creation of *Beyond Brokenness*. I thank the trees whose trunks and branches have become the pages you are holding in your hands; and the stars, the moon, and sun whose light nourished the trees; and the earth in whose darkness the seeds of the trees gestated and took root. Thank you to the rain that nurtured the trees and to the myriad creatures that nested and made their homes in the bark, branches, and leaves. Each of you is a part of this book too.

Acknowledgments

Beyond Brokenness is, in many ways, a tribute to my awesome parents who were two of the most wonderful human beings I have known. Their unstoppable creativity and love of inquiry continue to blossom through their children and grandchildren in many ways. To my brothers, one living and one whose death opened me to the great unknown, I offer appreciation and love.

Overflowing gratitude goes to those who tended the gardens, carried on with the many projects, kept things functioning, and cared for the animals here so I could take time to write: Kayt, Ildi, Russel, Arly, Deborah, Heather, Osella, Paul and Sarah, Mette, Helena, Christine, Susan, Lucy, Andy, Sharon and most especially Sonja—if not for her dedicated and consistent love for this 'aina during the last three years, the writing of this book would not have been possible.

I smile in gratitude for the many four-legged companions who brighten my days with their beaming eyes, wagging tails, purring, and bleating; and to the many birds whose songs are interwoven throughout these pages, including the mynah birds whose raucous chatter at dusk I have grown fond of, the orange-eyed roosters learning to crow, and the pueos[4] who circle the fields at night, screeching while searching for prey.

---

[4] Hawaiian owls.

I would also like to thank all of you who have given your valuable feedback, suggestions, and support. Your love and encouragement has meant a lot: Dove, Sahra, Sonja, Tao, Brooke, Jim, Susan, Jenni, Kayt, Cassandra, Tom, Aureya, Hrieth, Jaime, Joan, Christine, and Carolyn. Special thanks to Helena, who read and reread every word of the ever-changing versions several times and gave valuable feedback from the very beginning. Thank you for your patience, continual prodding, and gracious, loving encouragement and reflection.

I offer a song of thanks to Tom Joyce and Mary Ford-Grabowsky, whom I have yet to meet. Tom, whose introduction to the poem makes me laugh every time I read it, and Mary, who offered loving support in many ways and was a source of encouragement throughout the writing of this book. Respect and thanks to Michele Ryan, whom I did not have the opportunity to know.

I extend deep-abiding gratitude to Mirabai Starr for her foreword. Several years ago, during a seven-week retreat in Taos, New Mexico, a neighbor asked if I would accompany her to a memorial service that was happening within the hour. Having no idea who had died or where the service was taking place, I said, "Of course." Mirabai had just lost her fourteen-year-old daughter, Jenny, and was at the Hanuman Temple surrounded by hundreds of people offering words of condolence and sharing joyous memories of her beloved daughter. I remember seeing Mirabai standing with her mother in front of a large collage of photographs of Jenny who only days before had been vibrantly alive. She seemed to be holding everything, including the vast emptiness, as skillfully as a professional juggler juggling flaming torches of fire. Thank you, Mirabai, for making time in your very full life to write the foreword.

I offer my gratitude to all of you who sent letters and e-mails, sharing your broken-open hearts and gratitude, including those whose letters do not appear in the book, and to the many co-inquiring travelers of the way, retreatants, guests, and WWOOFers who have allowed me to be a part of your pathless journeys. I also wish to thank the many people who attended the councils and song circles, private sessions, and retreats I facilitated in the past twenty-four years.

I extend profound gratitude to my beloved teachers and mentors who have imparted to me their wisdom, love, honesty, humor, generosity, understanding, and ruthlessness. Immense gratitude also to the many unknown, unrecognized teachers who have profoundly touched my life: the aging black woman in Washington Square whose feet are bandaged with rags; the Mexican child whose stomach is empty, his hands too weak to pray; the limbless man in India, whose eyes glistened like black pearls and whose love I can still feel. All of you are woven through the words and empty spaces of these pages.

Thank you to Edna St. Vincent Millay, Audre Lorde, Joanna Macy, Emilie Conrad, Hildegard von Bingen, Rumi, Erich Fromm, John O'Donohue, Thich Nhat Hanh, Henry Wadsworth Longfellow, and the many, many poets, artists, and songwriters who have blessed my life with depth and beauty.

Special gratitude to Leilah Cornelia and Sherwin Soy and everyone else at Xlibris who was part of the creation of this book.

Foreword by Mirabai Starr

In *Beyond Brokenness*, Rashani Réa answers the call to dress the bones of her exquisite blessing of a poem in the colors of the human experience, revealing to a vast community of those who have suffered grief and loss the path to increased aliveness and mysterious joy. As a grief counselor, a bereaved mother, and a translator of the mystics, I will share this book as the philosopher's stone that it is, an alchemical tool for transmuting impossible sorrow into radiant peace.

I know about brokenness. And I am learning about the unbroken that rises, like light, like birdsong, like breath, from the wreckage. There are glimpses everywhere. This poem and this book, by Rashani, for example. They are the finger pointing to the moon. Look up. Look within.

Like Rashani, I have experienced an unusual number of losses in my life. Maybe you have too. From an early age, I began to taste the great mystery of death. Like Rashani, I endured the loss of my older brother, Matty, who died of a brain tumor when he was ten and I was seven. Like Rashani, I watched as something inside my parents died with their son; and our family, as I knew it, was transfigured by grief. As the years unfolded, other beloved relatives and close friends died. When I was fourteen, my first love, Phillip, was killed in a gun accident, which catapulted me into a life of prayer and meditation, irrevocably launching my spiritual quest.

Finally, the year I turned forty, the very day my first book came out, a translation of *Dark Night of the Soul* by the sixteenth-century Spanish saint John of the Cross, my fourteen-year-old daughter, Jenny, was killed in a car accident. I say "finally" not because I harbor any illusions that this will be the last loss I will have to bear, but because Jenny's death changed everything for me. Suddenly, the

Great Mystery I had been chasing all my life turned and swept me into its arms. I was plunged into the abyss, instantaneously intimate with the vast stillness and pulsing silence at which all my favorite mystics hint. So shaken I could not see my own hand in front of my face, I felt myself held in the invisible arms of a Love I had only dreamed of. Emblazoned with anguish, I found myself resting in fire. Drowning in despair, I surrendered and discovered I could breathe underwater.

So this was the state of profound suchness I had been searching for during all those years of rigorously cultivating a contemplative practice. This was the holy longing the saints had been talking about in poems that had broken my heart again and again. This was the sacred emptiness that put that small smile on the faces of the great sages. And I hated it. I didn't want vastness of being. I wanted my baby back.

But as Rashani reminds us, with tremendous tenderness, in the lines of her profound poem (page 171) and in the pages of her personal story, there is ultimately nowhere to hide when radical sorrow unravels the fabric of our lives. We can rage against the terrible unknown—and we will, for we are human and have these precious bodies and passionate hearts and complicated minds—or we can turn toward the cup, bow to the cupbearer, and say yes.

I didn't do it right away, nor did I sustain a continuous state of surrender, but I did learn to yield to my suffering, and in that submission, compassion for all suffering beings began to unexpectedly swell in my heart. My interdependence with all beings has never again been an abstract concept to me. I am viscerally aware of my debt to every blade of grass. These are a few of the unexpected blessings that emerged from the ashes of my loss. This is the growing relationship with the unbroken that has been given as the antidote to my brokenness.

And this is why Rashani's words speak so directly to my heart. What strikes me as most beautiful about her work is her ability to share the deeply human and sometimes unglamorous truth of sorrow and loss, insight and delight, and ultimately peace within that brokenness. Neither you nor I invented grief or are alone in our commitment and ability to transform through suffering. This book is an invitation to celebrate the ordinary, the connectedness to all, and the gloriously imperfect.

I have always been drawn to the perennial wise teachings that speak of the transformational power of suffering, and I have even made my living conveying these teachings to others. But I never needed them until my daughter died. Suddenly, anything that offered a glimpse of the unbroken became as essential as water, as vital as blood. Now I count myself among the many thousands of people who have read Rashani's words and wept with gratitude and relief; my own shattered heart has been seen and loved. Not in spite of my brokenness, but because of it. As Rashani says, "I decided to abandon the assumption that something is wrong if people are suffering."

On the contrary! Grief and loss are often the tender hands that lift off the armor from our limited false selves to reveal our glorious naked *true selves*. "That annihilating inoculation of holy aloneness stops us in our tracks," Rashani writes. "All paths disappear into this startling visitation, and the illusion of security is replaced by a vast groundlessness through which we have the opportunity to become servants of the compassionate, broken-open heart."

We're not referring to some rarified state reserved for long-dead saints and the occasional living master. Sacred wholeness is our birthright. Unbrokenness lies within the disappointments and delights of everyday life. In weeding the garden and burning the toast. In falling asleep alone or enfolded in the arms of another. In reading poetry instead of watching the news. In missing the grandmother you adored and becoming the father you never had. In weeping for the suffering of the oppressed, the degradation of the planet, the frozen finch who did not survive the winter in your own front yard. In singing, in rejoicing against all odds.

Recently, I taught a class called Death and Transformation at a seminary. I read Rashani's poem, and everyone wanted copies, which I made for them. I got to experience firsthand the power of "The Unbroken" as several others describe in this book. In *Beyond Brokenness*, Rashani has found the language—the language of words, of rhythm, of image and color, the language of love—to convey and celebrate the Great Mystery. Rashani knows how to get out of her own way and let the beauty come through her. By saying yes to the fire that illuminated the landscape of her own soul, Rashani is able to offer the rest of us hope for the transmutation of our suffering into a direct experience of *unbroken love*.

PART ONE

First there is a miracle

CHILDHOOD

*This is what it is
happily ever after
right in this moment.*

*Can we embrace brokenness
as an integral part of wholeness?*

I am mysteriously moved by the many phone calls, letters, and e-mails I have received and that continue to arrive, thanking me for and asking permission to publish this poem that I wrote in December 1991. Now, seventeen years later, invisible ribbons of wind are wrapping themselves through dancing tree branches as the full moon rises slowly. The persistence of the wind and a screeching owl usher me into silence. White irises and a black night moth illumined in darkness encourage me to write.

Love births quietly

My mother was a poet, a creator of Japanese gardens, a mosaicist, and a stained glass window artist and my father—a philosopher, an architect, a painter, and a professor of art history, aesthetics, and painting. With the exception of a car accident when I was four years old, minor scratches and bruises from falling off bicycles, and the occasional fall from trees and galloping horses, the first eleven years of my life were rather heavenly.

My oldest brother, Charlie, was seven years older than me and was my hero in many ways. My other brother, Bruce, is eleven months and eight days older than me. He too was my hero, in a different way. Bruce and I were in the same grade and sometimes the same class between kindergarten and high school. Apparently, I screamed so loud the day he left for kindergarten that at my mother's insistence, the school principal let me join the class. When we were young and our parents' friends asked us what we wanted to be when we grew up, Bruce would often say, "A saint." Though I wasn't quite sure what a saint *was*, I intuitively knew that it was not something to which I aspired. Charlie with certainty answered, "A guitarist." I dreamed of having an orphanage filled with children of all colors and ages, sizes and shapes and would often follow this by saying, "I *also* wanna be ambidextrous, bilingual, and bisexual." Early in life, I had an innate sense of wholeness and inclusiveness.

I have vivid memories of exploring the stone quarries where my mother carefully chose the rocks she used in her gardens and playing hide-and-seek in the nurseries with my brothers while my mother spoke to the nurserymen about maple trees, irises, and bamboo. With wonderment, having no idea that when I turned fifty I would spend two years rebuilding ancient stone walls and discovering the indescribable joy of spending five hours in the pouring rain moving and positioning three huge rocks, I watched my mother dance as she moved what to me at the time appeared to be enormous stone creatures, making them seem light as balsa wood. She explained to us the importance of emptiness, the space between rocks, trees, and the pond's edge and showed us how the eye naturally moves from the contour of one shape to another, without deliberate awareness. She introduced us to *shibui*, the Japanese word that embodies simplicity, understated elegance, and unobtrusive beauty. She shared wonderful examples to illustrate *shibui*, and I would drink in these stories word by word, mysteriously transported into the serenity of a Zen garden or silently imagining the evening light in the space between a blossoming cherry bough and a pine tree.

Sometimes we would help our mother dig bamboo from the shallow-rooted clumps along the sloping bank of my favorite creek a few miles from home. The bamboo nodes grew several inches per day, and my brothers and I were enamored with the miraculous qualities and diversity of nature.

I also remember sitting quietly in my mother's studio while she cut colored glass with a small dark green metal tool that had a diamond-edged blade at the end that rolled against the glass, making a scratching sound as it moved. She would turn the glass over, tap it a few times on the back, and I was amazed, each time, at how exactly the glass would break along the lines that she had carefully etched. Her precision fascinated me and held my attention for hours at a time. Her studio had a timeless quality and was as sacred to me as any temple or church, synagogue or mosque. I felt the presence of something beyond knowing and was acutely aware of an unnamable mystery as I sat quietly observing from a round soft cushion in the shade of the pepper tree, which appeared to be looking through the window from time to time, seemingly as touched as I was by the pure creativity that poured through my mother's hands.

I remember watching her making mosaics too. I loved the way the colorful tessera pieces sank into the thick glue and was thrilled when my mother grouted a completed mosaic. Sometimes she let me fill in the spaces between the tiles. Then, with long sweeping gestures and a damp sponge in her hand, she would cover the entire mosaic, making sure that every crack was filled. The design would disappear under an opaque film of grout, and I remember the excitement when, ten or fifteen minutes later, with a clean sponge, she would wipe off the extra grout and the colorful design would reappear in its entirety, more beautiful than before. Unbeknownst at the time, I was being gifted with one of many unspoken metaphors that would accompany me through many losses and challenges during the years to come.

My father designed the house where my family lived, in the foothills of Northern California, and hired Japanese carpenters to do the finishing work. Both of my parents shared a love and respect for Japanese culture. My father also designed a few other homes in the same vicinity, and I loved going with him to the job sites when he spoke with the engineers and builders. My fascination for architecture and building was spawned from those early days, watching him design and orchestrate the construction of spacious, elegant, and simple wooden, glass, and stone buildings. "Beauty affects us silently," he would say. He too had an understanding of *shibui*, and it showed in his buildings and paintings. I loved this word, *shibui*, perhaps because it was impossible to define. It was something I simply understood: a particular aesthetic that is beautiful in a simple, unflamboyant way and is precisely what it is meant to be without needing to be elaborated upon. *Shibui* is never complicated or contrived and leaves one with a deep feeling of stillness.

I also loved accompanying my father on field trips when he would take his college art-appreciation classes to museums in San Francisco and to the studios and homes of local artists. We visited painters, poets, potters, sculptors, and composers. These lively people shared their passion about the *creative process*, which was another invisible mystery.

Some of my most colorful memories are of visiting with Yanko Varda on his ferryboat in Sausalito. We often went to visit Varda on Sunday mornings to sail in the bay on his brightly painted sailboat. One time, he invited the entire African dance troupe for dinner, and that was an unforgettable night. His ferryboat was his home as well as his studio, and he made textured collages with a vivid assortment of cloths and unusual paper. In his kitchen, on the windowsills, were different colored bottles and pieces of stained glass, so even the light was filled with color around him.

I remember visiting Coit Tower where my father had painted murals with Diego Rivera years before I was born. His style of painting, back then, was different; and I loved noticing how creativity changed and evolved, even though creativity itself was impossible to locate. "*Who* or *what*[5] was

---

[5] This persistent question accompanied me for years, and as a senior in high school, I put together a book of collages and quotations about the creative process. The book is entitled *The Unfurling of an Artist*.

the source of creativity," I wondered, "that lives inside all of these artists and poets and composers?" Everything was art and vibrantly animated with life.

At the age of ten, when I told my father that I wanted to be a serious artist, he handed me a rapidograph pen, a box of charcoal, and several large pads of blank drawing paper and told me to draw a thousand hands. "Freedom is discipline" was the occasionally spoken and semiunderstood saying in those days. I took him seriously and began at once to draw hands: young and old hands, hands of all colors, physically different and dexterous hands, quiet and immobile hands, hands petting cats and playing guitars and pianos, hands holding protest signs in civil rights marches, hands curled into fists and open hands, hands holding knives and forks and chopsticks, hands playing chess and scrabble, hands underwater, hands covered in dirt.

I carefully studied my own hands when no one else was around, drew my left hand with my right and my right hand with my left. I was fascinated by my father's hands, which were dark brown in color, similar to my own. His right hand was like a Michelangelo sculpture, and his other hand, having been smashed in a car accident, had a different shape and texture. The surgeon decided to leave the metal pins in his arm since the break was so serious. I don't recall ever thinking that his left hand should have been any different than it was. There was a strange beauty and perfection in his imperfectness.

Two and a half years later, I brought him more than ten drawing pads filled with drawings. I had spent nearly thirty months studying and drawing hands. "Here are the thousand hands," I said. He looked at every drawing, commenting from time to time while nodding his head. Though I was expecting him to offer his usual, somewhat formal critique, he instead asked me which ones I most enjoyed drawing and asked me to share what I had discovered while studying hands. He loved the aliveness of questions and knew that the right question had the capacity to unearth the wisdom that existed in every person. He asked questions that elicited something deeper than pride or gratification. He genuinely wanted to know what it had been like for me during those two and a half years silently observing hands. An artist himself, influenced by the writing of Henry and William James, Bertrand Russell, and other philosophers, my father was interested in my inner experience, the awareness with which I perceived, as well as the actual drawings. The discipline he valued was not only in concentration, which he said anyone could perfect with enough practice, but the art of being aware and present to each moment, as it is. "Being a technician is not enough," he would say. This was my first conscious experience of meditative inquiry with another person.

It was an unexpected moment when my father informed me that I could now burn all of the drawings. "It's not always the final product that counts," he said. At first I wanted to protest and keep the drawings forever, wanted to frame them, show them to all of my friends and save them for my children. He continued, "We don't own what is created through us." As I watched page after page of my cherished drawings curl into pieces of charred ash, I was silently aware of something, *a presence*, that could never be burned.

My parents wanted their children to see and listen deeply, unencumbered by anyone else's opinions or even by our own ideas or interpretations. They were constantly inviting us to look at things directly, to listen more attentively; and they created endless opportunities for us to explore the invisible mosaic of awareness, reminding us often of the empty space between objects. My father spoke with passion about philosophy, music, and the *aesthetic experience*; and my mother, through her love of Taoism, poetry, and nature, pointed to the moon in a different way. Now, four and a half decades later, I realize that they were both, in their unique ways, referring to consciousness itself, which is neither the one perceiving nor that which is perceived; they were gently alluding to that which contains and is contained by the myriad contents of awareness, without ever choosing to name it.

Let it be nameless,
whatever creates union.
Night melts into dawn.

Rashani

Childhood

I remember several intimate experiences from my childhood: the sense of dissolving into everything, where I was no longer a girl or an artist or anyone at all. There was simply a sense of being present, regardless of what was happening. I remember sitting in the garden one Sunday morning, when I was six and a half years old, while my father painted my portrait. It was difficult to stay in one position for long periods; by the time the portrait was complete, late that same afternoon, I had only one braid left as the other one had undone itself while I ran wildly through the garden and went splashing in the creek, playing with the baby goats that lived behind my bedroom. I remember being fascinated by the sound of charcoal on canvas and wanted to know how it was that with a few movements of his hand, my father could capture the essence of another's face or body on a two-dimensional space. I was mesmerized by his capacity to make color into eyes and cheeks and foreheads, into still lifes, landscapes, and abstract symphonies of shapes.

He often played Mozart, Schubert, Prokofiev, or Satie when he painted; and I can still remember, a few years later, disappearing into Satie's *Trois Gymnopédies* while my father was stretching a large canvas. I loved watching him pour turpentine into the two small silver cups that clipped onto his palette and how carefully he mixed colors while humming Mozart or Schubert, whose music he loved and knew by heart. Each timeless moment melted into the next.

Occasionally, my father read us bedtime stories. Sometimes he read to us from the *Grimm's Fairy Tales* and other times he read from Colette, one of his favorite writers. He introduced us to her book, *My Mother's House*. Later, when we traveled through Europe, he read us *My Family and Other Animals* by Gerald Durrell and introduced us to the writing of Joseph Campbell. His library was filled with books about art, literature, and architecture, and he had a particularly large section for his favorite philosophers.

Sometimes when our parents were gone, Bruce and I would climb with our friends up on top of the tall wooden bookshelves and jump down on the other side, landing on my parents' king-size bed, laughing with delight, screeching joyously as we rolled onto the floor as make-believe creatures or as secret spies chasing an imaginary enemy.

It is the ordinary that I have loved and celebrated for as long as I can remember. From the time I was seven or eight years old, each morning before breakfast, my brothers and I were invited to find three miracles. We would walk quietly into the garden, each drawn in a different direction. During breakfast, we shared our discoveries. Little did I know how meaningful this simple practice was and how profoundly it would impact my entire life. We were discovering divinity and cultivating presence, though no words were used to describe it as such. Sometimes it was in the sound of a woodpecker boring into a walnut tree, the sharing of a dream, the song of the creek after a night of rain, the magnificence of a single dew drop, the splendor of a flower or a spider's web, the way light sifts through bamboo leaves, how our bare feet felt when walking on dry leaves, or how subtly the feel of our skin changed when we noticed the wind more attentively. Finding sanctity in the most ordinary things, we were invited, day after day, to experience our inseparability from the infinite expressions of life.

Even death was included in our "miracle game." When hummingbirds and sparrows flew into the large windows that overlooked our garden, we would find their tiny bodies motionless on the ground. One time we found three baby raccoons whose mother had been killed. We nursed them with a small plastic bottle for several days and were heartbroken to find them dead one morning. "How could the absence of life be a miracle?" I wondered. "It simply is because it is," my brothers assured me. Death seemed like part of the imperfect perfection of everything. We could find nothing that was not in some way miraculous. No miracle was less or more important than another. Each was totally unique, imbued with its own suchness and undeniably interconnected. There was no delineation between ordinary and extraordinary, beautiful and ugly, or even between life and death. There was nothing for us to believe, reject, or obtain. We celebrated one another's discoveries without competition or comparison as we gobbled our cereal or scrambled eggs on toast. These precious mornings were graced with simplicity, joy, and wishlessness.[6] Nature and our nighttime dreams were the laboratories in which we discovered the mysteries of being

---

[6] Other names for *wishlessness* are unconditioned presence, nondual awareness, original wisdom, and "simply this." In this space, nothing is lacking and nothing is needed in order to enhance it.

alive. Nothing in nature was trying to be any different than it was, and I noticed the same thing in my dreams. Awareness itself was a miraculous thing. Well, not exactly a *thing* because it couldn't be located. Becoming aware of awareness was a never-ending river. What *is* it? Where did awareness come from?

During the summers, after I turned eight years old, my mother held art classes three days a week. Several of the neighborhood children arrived with their lunches and art materials neatly packed in large brown paper bags. A few friends who lived farther away would be dropped off by their mothers, excited by and welcomed into the ever-unfolding journey of discovery. Sometimes my mother poured us each a cup of tea and invited us to sit in silence while watching irises open in the morning sunlight. Sometimes we drew them while they opened. We made wire sculptures, collages, papier-mâché animals, mosaics out of dried beans and split peas and pebbles gathered from pebble beach. We hand-lettered books of poetry, made plaster casts of one another's faces, learned how to use oil and acrylic paints and different kinds of paintbrushes and pens.

I remember the time that several of us made mosaics as gifts for our parents. We had spent many weeks carefully gluing colorful dried lentils, peas, and beans onto plywood backing. We decided to leave them behind my mother's studio until the end of the summer, as a surprise. We hid them under a long wide wooden bench, pushed way to the back where they touched the wall. As summer drew to an end, we excitedly crawled under the bench to retrieve our works of art. Much to our disappointment, the chickens and mice had discovered our mosaics and had pecked and nibbled off many of the beans, peas, and lentils. Impermanence was everywhere.

Everything was a discovery, a sustained inquiry of sorts into existence itself and into our relationships with one another and especially into ourselves. We were invited, again and again, to observe without judgment or comparison, to cultivate an observation that went beyond right or wrong, good or bad. Curiosity was our saving grace.

I detested fourth grade. How and what we explored and were allowed to discover on our own at home was so much more exciting than what we learned at school. Sometime during the autumn of that year, before I got kicked out of the Brownies for pushing Missy Moses into a swimming pool, I went on a field trip with the Brownies to the Stanford Hospital. While we were standing hand in hand with our partners, watching blood being mixed up in a test tube, my partner, Cindy Anderson, fainted. She fell limply to the tile floor while still holding my hand. Nurses immediately rushed into the room, and Cindy was put on a stretcher and taken away. No one wanted to sit next to her on the way home. Everyone thought she had died. I was intrigued and wanted to know where she had gone. For the following weeks, I incessantly asked questions about unconsciousness and had flashbacks of the car accident I had been in four years previously. "Where had my father and Cindy gone?" I kept asking. I knew that their bodies were still breathing, so they couldn't have been dead. "Was memory different from consciousness?" I wondered. Did consciousness *contain* memory? I longed to know about the invisible realms and wanted to know where dreams came from. I remember lying in bed sometimes, late at night, unable to sleep, wondering what would have existed if the universe had never been created. My mind was horrified at the thought! I could not imagine an empty cosmos. I wanted to know who or what had created everything or if all of life was the dreaming of a larger, infinite source. "Was I breathing or was something else breathing through me?"

None of my teachers at school would answer my questions. Instead, they suggested to my parents that I see the school counselor. He was a rather unfriendly and nervous man who smoked cigarettes during recess, smelled like tobacco, and wore grey clothes. My friends had unanimously decided that anyone who was so unfriendly couldn't possibly be able to help us or answer our questions. So I had no desire to see the school counselor.

One day my mother found me playing in the creek when I was supposed to have been at school. Instead of punishing me, she asked me why I wasn't at school. I told her how disappointed I was that none of my teachers had time for my questions and begged her to not send me back to school. When she asked me what I would like to do instead, I replied, even though I didn't own a horse, "I want to ride my horse in the mountains." I also shared with her that since Cindy had fainted in the hospital, I was having unusual dreams and spent time every day preoccupied with memories of the car accident I'd been in at the age of four.

The following month, for my ninth birthday, I was given a horse. I named her Norkinu—*unicorn* spelled backward, almost—and was allowed to ride in the mountains and creeks without going to school. Norkinu was a stocky, gentle creature, part Clydesdale and part quarter horse. The truant officer and counselor called regularly, as well as the school principal. In spite of their insistence that I would be much better off at school and with psychiatric help, my mother explained that I would not be returning to school until I had made peace with the car accident.

My mother made art materials abundantly available and encouraged me to draw, sculpt, and paint my dreams and memories. One of her closest friends was a Jungian analyst and another dear friend of hers, Charlotte, was a Lakota Sioux medicine woman from the Rosebud Indian Reservation in Carter, South Dakota. When Charlotte heard about my dreams, she sent me my first medicine bundle. In it were sand crystals from South Dakota and a small white-and-brown bear carved from a piece of animal bone. She told me that the bear would help me go inside where I would find the answers to all of my questions. For several months, I drew, painted, and made collages, sometimes of my dreams and memories and other times of animals and people and trees. I rode Norkinu every afternoon and was usually home by dark. The mountains and creeks, redwood forests and apple orchards sang with me as I rode bareback into the winter afternoons. One of my favorite friends in those days was named Claudia. On weekends, we would ride all day and share a picnic lunch. Once, we discovered a wonderful lake high in the hills and rode our horses into the water. They snorted and moved awkwardly through the water hyacinths and floating lily pads, their front hooves splashing and chopping the dark green water.

Bruce and I were given a choice to wash dishes or write poetry that year. Sometimes I had fun washing dishes, and other times I loved writing, especially haiku and tanka poetry, to which my mother's friend, Lucille Nixon, had introduced me. In the mid-1950s, Lucille became the first foreigner to be honored at the Imperial New Year's Poetry Reading offered annually by the emperor and empress of Japan. Lucille touched an aliveness in me that was deeper than usual, particularly when she shared poems that she had translated from Japanese into English. She was working on a book called *Sounds from the Unknown*; and when I was with her, I experienced poetry emerging as magically as bamboo shoots from the hidden earth, the unknown. I could feel *shibui* in poetry too. Little by little, I began to befriend the unknown, and my obsession with unconsciousness eventually faded. Lucille invited me to write poems about my dreams, and when the dreams were put into seventeen or thirty-one syllables (haiku and tanka),[7] they were suddenly less frightening. She became

---

[7] Two traditional forms of Japanese poetry.

a special friend who helped me tremendously in bridging the visible and invisible worlds.

One day, in late spring, I was ready to return to school. I asked to be put in a different class and was delighted by my new teacher, Ms. Fincher, who introduced us to Native American history and let us chew gum on Fridays. She drove a bright yellow Plymouth convertible with a dent on the rear fender and was fully supportive of me riding my horse to school. She was one of those rare teachers who sees the essence of every child, who lovingly encourages them to blossom however they will, and in whose presence everyone feels valued, special, and equal. "Uniqual." Ms. Fincher's classroom was a dynamic, vivacious place. I made many new friends that spring.

As much as I enjoyed school, I was happy when summer arrived again so I could attend the classes taught by my mother. A few of my newly made friends joined the class, and Vida Shapiro came all the way from Skyline Boulevard. On the first day of that second summer, my mother shared with us a quote by Erich Fromm. I was nine years old at the time, and Bruce was ten. My sixteen-year-old brother, Charlie, was in Mexico with his teacher's family, studying flamenco guitar. We were given a week to memorize the words and were asked to write a poem about what Fromm's words meant for us. Though the actual wording may be different, this is what I remember it as being:

If you perceive only the surface of things, you will only understand the differences that separate you. If you penetrate to the core, you will begin to understand yourself and all of mankind.

My poem was about my girlfriend, Adeola, who was from Nigeria. My brother's was about a walnut. Maggie Spencer's poem was about a lake. Though I don't remember the content of any of the other poems, they were each completely different and very personal explorations of perception, of seeing beneath outer surfaces into what was essential and hidden. With the same excitement and absence of competition that we had engendered during our miracle-sharing mornings, my brother and I shared our poems with each other and with our friends. I loved hearing others' poems and still recall that on that particular morning we were sitting outside, beneath the weeping willow tree, next to a curving tier of blooming periwinkle. I became Adeola as I wrote the poem and understood the essence of Fromm's words.

The Civil Rights Movement was growing. I didn't understand the extremes of injustice and felt protective and concerned about anyone who was marginalized. The following year, I had to stay after school for giving Mario Garriano a karate chop on the back of his neck. He had been squirting a squirt gun and throwing rocks at Adeola's little brother. When I saw Mario teasing and hurting Ajani, I was outraged. I had not yet learned the importance of nonviolence. All I knew was that someone was being wrongfully treated, and very few others dared to confront the school bullies. Around the time of the great March on Washington, in July of 1964, my brother Bruce and I were taken out of school one day, shortly after lunch. Our mother came to get us, saying that we were going to see a great man. He was leading a protest march, accompanied by Joan Baez, in East Palo Alto. People of all colors, but mostly African Americans, lined the streets for miles and miles, and Martin Luther King Jr. spoke passionately about equal rights. That day was a turning point in my life. I can still remember singing "We Shall Overcome" and seeing the tears pouring down many people's faces, including my own. I knew that I wanted to sing for justice and wanted my artwork to somehow reflect my concerns. Bruce and I began donating our woodcut prints to local exhibitions that were fund-raising for equal housing rights for people of color, and this was the beginning of my impassioned calling to creative social activism.

The summer between fifth and sixth grade was a memorable one. The redwood picnic table under the wisteria vine was often covered with books of poetry. My friends and I were invited to choose our favorites. My brother loved T. S. Elliot, Rilke, and Gerard Manley Hopkins. Larry Richardson was fascinated by the words of Dylan Thomas and Emily Dickinson. Naomi Jacobson was in love with e. e. cummings and Robert Frost. After lunch, we would sit quietly by the creek or under the huge eucalyptus trees or by the waterfall that my mother had made. We didn't need to understand *why* we were drawn to particular poets or their words. We were simply given the freedom to discover what we loved.

That summer, in the hollow root of a bay tree that protruded out over the creek, I began memorizing "Renascence," my favorite poem by Edna St. Vincent Millay. By the end of the summer, I knew the first twenty lines by heart and completed the memorization of the entire poem five and a half years later, as a sophomore in high school. I still remember discovering this amazing poem and making the vow to memorize every stanza. Edna's words flowed through me, into places that I could not describe, touching me the way moonlight touches wind. Her words moved and took me with them, from the relative into the absolute, from a painful moment into eternity, as effortlessly as breathing. Her poem invited me into, through, and beyond human suffering, to the incomprehensible understanding of deathlessness, as gently as a slowly opening iris; she captured the inseparability of form and formlessness, life and death, whether it was in her words or in the spaces between the words, I didn't exactly know.

I wonder now, looking back, how it was that I could have understood what she was saying at such a young age. Perhaps I didn't. Perhaps it was the sense of disappearing that I loved so much. Every time I read the poem, soon into the second stanza, I would become aware of an exquisite tenderness and melting, a sense of liquefying into nothing and everything simultaneously. It was as if this poem was a doorway into unconditioned awareness and a celebratory reunion with the radiant identity of Oneness. Here again was the sense of wishlessness. "Renascence" also gave me solace after I heard about the tragic death of my dear friend, Lucille Nixon.

After Edna imagines being dead, she cries out and is reborn. This is a small part of the poem:

> *The grass, a-tiptoe at my ear,*
> *Whispering to me I could hear;*
> *I felt the rain's cool finger-tips*
> *Brushed tenderly across my lips,*
> *Laid gently on my sealèd sight,*
> *And all at once the heavy night*
> *Fell from my eyes and I could see,*
> *A drenched and dripping apple-tree,*
> *A last long line of silver rain,*
> *A sky grown clear and blue again.*
> *And as I looked a quickening gust*
> *Of wind blew up to me and thrust*
> *Into my face a miracle*
> *Of orchard-breath, and with the smell,*
> *I know not how such things can be!*
> *I breathed my soul back into me.*

Everything in this poem was vibrantly alive: the dripping apple trees, whispering grass blades, the quickening gust of wind, and so much more. Every living being seemed like a part of the same sentient, nonlocal awareness of which my own personal awareness was but an immeasurable speck.

Even death had aliveness to it in this poem. "How was this possible?" I pondered. When I first read "Renascence" I had no idea that it would accompany me through my life, as a companion.

*"The lamps are different
but the light is the same."*

—Sufi saying

In sixth grade, three friends came to our house on Mondays, Wednesdays, and Fridays early in the mornings and walked to school with Bruce and me. We loved the paths through the eucalyptus grove and the hill covered with buckeye trees and wild ferns. We often looked for snakes and toads on our way home from school and loved the ponds where the salamanders and frogs laid their jellylike eggs.

During those mornings, my mother introduced us to a new and exciting world. With warm cups of tea in our hands, we learned about ancient mythology and different cultures.

We loved hearing about African tribes, clans from Papua New Guinea and Borneo, Native American shamans, and Australian Aboriginal healers. I was fascinated by the art of these tribal people and got hold of as many books as I could to learn more. My mother read to us, and we spent time looking on our own at other books that had colorful photographs and descriptive captions.

In the spring of that year, we learned about Judaism, Jainism, Christianity, Shintoism, Taoism, Buddhism, Islam, and Hinduism. We took turns reading from the Torah and Old Testament, the Upanishads and Koran, the Tao Te Ching and other sacred texts. Each was presented to us as a unique and beautiful expression of sacred wisdom. My mother believed that equally as important as food and shelter to all human beings was the connection with the divine. She said there were many names for the invisible mystery that existed in all living things and suggested that perhaps one day we would be drawn to a particular religion or path. "Or," she added, "perhaps you will see the beauty in all of the expressions of love and choose to celebrate the diversity of the One." A common concern of all great mythologies and religions, she told us, was the dynamic relationship between life and death. We discussed the difference between faith and belief, talked about Buddha, Quan Yin, Christ, Krishna, Lakshmi, Mohammed, and Lao Tsu; and suddenly the world felt much bigger than before.

Childhood

Bruce and I memorized poems, listened to music, were given writing assignments, and were encouraged to perceive in different ways. We were invited to look at nature, at each other, at prisms and empty space, at dead birds, to look at ourselves, and at the most ordinary things like tree stumps, garbage cans, and faucets. We were encouraged to observe details and shadows, hues and colors and to notice where one object ended and another began. We discussed the difference between looking and seeing. We were asked to draw what we saw and to become aware of emptiness and spatial relationships.

Often we had a dead quail or coot in our freezer or any road-killed birds that we found on our walk home from school. We marveled at their motionless bodies and wondered where life went when it was no longer inside the animal. We looked carefully at their feathers, beaks, faces, and talons and drew what we saw. We were seeing life and death as part of the same fabric. We discovered that each of us perceived and portrayed things differently. We discussed perception and took turns being perceived by one another. We asked questions about the one perceiving and the one who was being perceived. Sometimes we were asked to pinch our thumbs and forefingers together, to make a tiny diamondlike space to look through, one eye at a time, and to notice if and how that changed our perception of reality.

Childhood | 75

My oldest brother, Charlie, was a flamenco, blues, and classical guitarist. He introduced me to Woody Guthrie and Bob Dylan, Segovia and Sabicas, many wonderful Spanish composers, and lots of blues and jazz musicians. He often played me to sleep with his newest flamenco assignments. "Charlie" was short for Charles Christopher. He had a motorcycle, and when I turned eleven, I was allowed to ride with him as long as I wore a helmet. For his eighteenth birthday, I painted his helmet with bright colors.

The summer he went to Mexico, I missed him terribly and counted the days until his return. Charlie was left-handed, and I remember the way his left hand curled around the pen when he wrote. It was different from the way the rest of my family held a pen or pencil. He returned from Mexico with a small cardboard box filled with amethyst and quartz crystals and an especially beautiful piece of translucent dark obsidian streaked with what he had been told was volcanic ash. Charlie knew how much I cherished rocks, and later that summer, he helped me build a shallow wooden box for my rock collection. I asked him how the amethyst crystals got their color. "The same way the birds got their songs," he replied. The conversation ended there, as there was really nothing more to say. Life was teeming with miracles, and I knew without knowing that we were all infinitesimal pieces of a breathing, infinite puzzle.

Charlie's dream was to travel to Spain and study flamenco guitar. After graduating from high school, he got a job in the local hardware store and earned enough money for his trip to Spain. Though excited for him, I was also sad that he was leaving home. He was my best friend, and I couldn't imagine what life would be like without him. He taught me how to listen in new ways and how to play the guitar. He was patient with me as I struggled with arpeggios and new chords.

I remember the time I dug my pet tortoise up from the earth while she was still hibernating. My tortoises were in a large enclosure outside of Charlie's bedroom. He was obviously home that day, looking out his window at that particular moment. I was so excited that spring had arrived, and I wanted Edwina, the mother tortoise, to see the gigantic purple irises around the pond. Charlie overheard me talking to her and watched me as I carried Edwina into the front garden. I probably tried to pry her eyes open in my zeal and innocence, all of seven or eight years old. The other tortoises woke naturally from their hibernation that spring, but Edwina never got to see the irises or eat another handful of crunchy lettuce from my hand. I felt terrible for weeks when I realized that I had killed a precious creature. Charlie bought me another tortoise and explained that all living things have their own rhythms. "Like music," he explained. Edwina's death was a shocking awakening for me, and I have remembered it often.

Charlie played his guitar many hours a day and was invited to play at parties and weddings and other social events. I loved watching his hands move magically across the strings of his guitar. He had a long shelf filled with records, and on the weekends, we often listened to music together. My parents' music was classical, which I loved, and Charlie's music collection was a whole new discovery of sound. He listened to Leadbelly and Dizzy Gillespie, Blind Lemon Jefferson, Jack Teagarden, Dave Brubeck, and many other musicians whose names I don't remember. I was as intrigued by the names of the musicians as I was by their music. Charlie taught me about improvisation and syncopation and explained that blues and jazz originated from folk songs and plantation music of early African Americans, some of whom had been slaves. He must have known every song by Bob Dylan, and if he didn't, he could figure it out. I was so proud of my big brother. His love of music was contagious; and when he left for Spain, I played Rodrigo's *Concerto de Aranjuez* over and over and over, interspersed with Bob Dylan, Harry Belafonte, Joan Baez, and Peter, Paul and Mary. The *Concerto de Aranjuez* was the first work that Rodrigo had written for guitar and orchestra. With such passion, Charlie had described to me the three parts of the concerto, and sometimes I cried during the second movement when the music becomes slow and quiet. It touched me in a deep way, and I couldn't explain it to anyone but Charlie.

Shortly after my twelfth birthday, Charlie left for Spain. I still remember what he was wearing when we drove him to the San Francisco airport. He flew to Los Angeles and took a boat to Barcelona where he continued his adventure with a handful of friends he met on the boat. They hitchhiked through Spain and arrived in Madrid in late January. He visited many guitar makers, in Seville, Grenada, Barcelona, Malaga, and Madrid, and finally found the guitar he had been dreaming of. Light golden wood with ebony black pegs. I missed Charlie but was happy to hear about his discoveries and adventures and was waiting impatiently for June. My father had decided to take a sabbatical, and we were going to meet Charlie in Spain and travel together for a year throughout Europe. My father was writing a book on European art and architecture and wanted to take us to the places that he was photographing for his book.

Charlie was a luminous sun around which my young heart joyously orbited. I spent time each day either writing to him or pressing flowers and leaves from the garden, cutting his favorite newspaper articles from the *San Francisco*

Chronicle or making collages for him with colorful paper and feathers. In early February, I bundled all of the gifts into a package and carefully wrote his name and address on the box. I was so excited that he would soon receive my colorful creations of love.

We are made gentle by love.

Rashani

The following week, Bruce and I walked to school as usual, and the day seemed unusually still. We had both heard Charlie's cat howling during the night, which she had never done before. Tammy was a calm creature who rarely made a sound. On the way to school, we wondered why Tammy suddenly needed to cry. The eeriness of it struck me as we walked along the high bank of the dry steep ridge across the road from school. The question hung suspended in the unknown spaces between my thoughts as Bruce and I went our ways down the open corridors to our separate classrooms.

A few hours later, we were both called to the principal's office. Our parents were standing outside beneath the large oak tree that hung over the parking lot. Though happy to see them, I felt something ominous hovering in the air. We drove home in silence and sat together in the garden beneath the leafless wisteria vine whose lavender clusters were perennial miracles year after year. Suddenly, the absence of the lavender flowers seemed more naked, more empty than usual. There was nervousness in my parents' voices, and finally the truth was spoken as they shared the telegram that had arrived earlier that morning.

Charlie had been found dead in Madrid.

Two weeks later, the unopened package I had sent him was returned. I stood at the mailbox, frozen, holding an enormous expression of love that was never received.

In the late sixties, a few years after Charlie's death, my mother wrote a short poem:

> *The earth falls away*
> *on the third of May*
> *so love every moment*
> *of winter.*

I often wondered why she had chosen the third of May. What was the significance of that day? Occasionally I asked her. In her unsentimental way, she would smile and say, "Just love every moment, especially in winter when the trees are bare and the days are short." After a sip or two of tea, she would continue, "There is only this moment. Nothing else, darling! That's all there is. Simply this!"

One of her favorite sayings was "Nothing matters but everything counts."

May third remained a mystery.

Now news travels fast, in cyberspace corridors, spun into a thousand directions with the push of one button. Back then, urgent messages were sent as telegrams. I watched my parents shatter silently after the death telegram arrived that February morning in 1965. The cause of Charlie's death was accidental asphyxiation. His landlord and teacher, Antonio Santiago, knowing that the gas heater was broken, had told my brother not to turn it on. He promised that it would be fixed by the end of the week. Charlie had not turned on the heater.

My breathing froze on the in-breath that long ago February morning. A scalpel of ice cut into my flesh and soul. My mind stopped, as it does every time with the news of death. Impaled by the words glaring plainly from a small rectangular piece of paper, I journeyed with Charlie into the vastness, into the bardos[8] of timelessness while the formless unknown curled around me like a molting snake. My pubescent body folded into itself in an instant and is still unfurling, forty-three years later. More like a banner

---

[8] Bardo literally means "in between." In Tibetan Buddhism, the realm of the afterlife is called the world of the bardo.

now, dancing, being shaped by the winds of life and love, birth and death, inhaling and exhaling, laughing and letting tears pour when they do.

After years of inner unrest, our mother informed us one morning that she was going to Spain, to forgive the man who had unintentionally killed her son. Up until the day when she showed up on his doorstep with a bouquet of flowers, Señor Santiago had denied the fact that he had turned on the broken heater. My mother's presence, devoid of blame or contempt, allowed the truth to be revealed. Her broken-open heart brought this man literally to his knees. There was no drama and no suppressing of feelings. Her compassion was a natural offering, nothing special, from one who had looked clearly into reality with a discerning heart-eye of wisdom. She embodied the simple realization that occurs in one who is able to distinguish between *what is* and the judgmental voice inside that is constantly interpreting reality. She didn't consider herself a spiritual person per se, but simply one who was willing to relinquish a position if it allowed for the bigger picture to be seen. She had a matter-of-factness with which it was impossible to disagree. Through her directness and clarity, I discovered the tender power of mercy and decided to abandon the assumption that something is wrong if people are suffering. There was no need to add to the human condition by making it into a problem.

I watched my parents live one day at a time, rarely speaking of Charlie, their firstborn child. They turned inward, turned more deeply toward art and poetry, silence and beauty. They spoke of *wu wei*[9] and were each drawn toward the nameless Mystery in different ways. At the time, innocently arrogant in my limited perspective of life, I accused them of living in denial. I wanted to hear their cries of anguish, to know the deep lament that I sensed when I looked into their eyes. I longed to know what they felt when they awoke every morning to the absence of my brother, their beloved son. There were no words for the hollowness that couldn't be filled. I lost not only my brother, but some part of my parents as well.

So much for miracles.

---

[9] Known in Taoism as "effortless action," also translated as "creative quietude" or the art of letting be.

ANOTHER PERSPECTIVE

A white silken scarf?
No, a remnant of moonlight
on the garden path.

My father's alcoholism had been hidden from me until Charlie's death. I gradually discovered the well-guarded secret by piecing together the car accidents, my mother's fear of letting us drive with him at night, and the broken promises, missed dinners, and unexplained arguments. My father was not a cruel drunkard, but he was dangerous every time he insisted on driving while inebriated. At the age of four, I was with him in a serious accident in which his left arm was ripped off by an oncoming car. In a subsequent car accident, he lost the sight of his left eye. I also remember the time he returned late at night, not knowing if he had hit a tree or a person. As the years passed, I grew enraged by his hypocrisy, unpredictability, and the ongoing pain he caused his family. In my early twenties, I refused to see him for a year due to a particularly terrifying experience. My childhood was a mixture of miracles, exquisite beauty, and recurring horrors. I remember saying to a friend, "If I can turn the hatred I have for my father into love and forgiveness, it will be the greatest feat of my lifetime."

Many of my friends had at least one alcoholic parent. There was a joke in the Buddhist community back then about it being the incognito recovery program for adult children of alcoholics. As I looked more compassionately into the nature of addiction, I became increasingly aware of its pervasive characteristics: denial, dishonesty, secrecy, the pretense of painlessness, and the shame that accompanies failure and brokenness. I saw it as a symptom, a crying out, from the depths of unattended anguish. I knew no one, including myself, who was exempt from some form of addiction. Whether it was to perfection, suffering, work, arrogance, pride, or alcohol and drugs, the habit originated from the same place. Observing another's forgiveness or witnessing someone else's mercy is different from the direct experience itself. Many of the premature attempts to forgive my father had come from a sense of obligation and had backfired in my face. When I saw his vulnerability and pain after the death of my mother, the veils of blame and judgment simply disappeared. Forgiveness flowered spontaneously. It was my turn to see from the wordless place of the broken-open heart, as I had watched my mother do several years before. Forgiveness, like love, is not something we *do* but is a natural current of energy, an effortless outcome of being the "other" long enough to dispel the illusion of separation. When judgment ceases, reality can be seen.

Love isn't something we do.
It simply moves through our being
reshaping us again and again
until all falseness has gone to seed
and the fragile husks
of who we are
fall away
or break into prayer
becoming kindling
for the long winters.

Rashani

Another Perspective

During the last seven years of my father's life, even though he continued to drink for five of those years, we shared a loving and honest relationship. I discovered a man whose humanness, humility, love, and authenticity allowed me to perceive miracles in a different way. Living without blame and judgment was a miracle in itself, not to mention staying present with the discomfort of uncertainty and not knowing. I was amazed that in the midst of situations that once made me want to walk away or cry, I was able to find peace. In the very heart of ambiguity and pain itself was the innocence and wishlessness I had known as a young child.

*If we could read the secret history of our enemies,
we would find in each man's life sorrow
and suffering enough to disarm all hostility.*

—Henry Wadsworth Longfellow

FRANCE

*Is it curse or grace,
entering the labyrinth
of the broken heart?*

Three years after Charlie's death, my family moved to Massachusetts. Our home in California felt like an empty shell, and we unanimously decided that it was time to leave. My father got a job as head of the art department at a college in Boston. I was also teaching art, at the age of sixteen, in the town of Ipswich and raising money for war-injured Vietnamese children and for children on the Rosebud Indian Reservation in South Dakota.

Bruce was chosen as number two in the draft lottery and did not want to be part of the war in Vietnam, so my father broke his tenure contract and the four of us moved to England. My parents bought a beautiful house in Hampshire, between Salisbury and Winchester; and on Sunday mornings, we sometimes drove to Brockwood Park to hear Krishnamurti.

It was my parents' dream to create an art school in the south of France. For three years, they went to France several times a year, looking for a place to settle and create the school. After the eighth or ninth trip, my mother was feeling discouraged. My father, determined to find the perfect place, set out one last time, on his own. I don't think it was self-determination so much as following an inner guidance and trusting the Tao of his dreams.

My parents had visited nearly every province in France, and this time, my father was headed for the Pyrenees, near the Spanish border. He said he would call us as soon as he arrived. A day earlier than expected, the phone rang; and it was my father calling to say that he had found the most beautiful valley, several hundred kilometers from his destination. A wild storm had forced him to stop driving, and he stayed the night in a small village, near the medieval city of Cahors on the Lot River. When he awoke the next morning, he *knew* that he had found the dream of many years. Or the dream had found him. Within three months, my parents settled in the Lot Province, near the village of Labastide-Murat. Bruce and I joined them often and began helping renovate an old stone barn for the school.

I was living in England attending art college, where I met the man who later became my husband. Martin had just spent seven years in a spiritual community and was on his way to India. He was the same age as Charlie, and we shared a deep love.

Two weeks after my twenty-second birthday, I gave birth to a gorgeous little boy and returned to France to be near my family. My mother had found a farmhouse near the school-to-be with a stone tower and barn for $7,000. The tile roofs were old and crumbling, the floors were mostly rotten, the chimney had collapsed, and the windows and doors were gone. It never had plumbing, and the electrical wires were dangerously old and had been eaten away in several places by rats. It was love at first sight!

For the first year, before the water meter was installed, I gathered water from a spring and washed diapers in a narrow trough where many of the local women washed their family's clothes. For two months, I worked five days a week with a group of local roofers and learned the art of roofing. Every three hours, I stopped to breast-feed my baby who was being cared for by my mother. It was *not* a common thing to see a woman on a roof in the south of France.

In my bones and memory, I knew about the vocal lament known as keening—the improvised cry that was once prevalent in Ireland, as well as in other cultures.

The acoustics of underground spaces and the fluidity and freedom of water called out the keening in me. I began my days, often before dawn, sounding and toning, sometimes with friends, in the ancient caves and stone cisterns near our small hamlet in France, but mostly alone, near rivers and streams, where my cries felt healthy and welcomed. There was often an indefinable moment when the cry turned mysteriously into song. Sometimes I felt that I was weeping for my parents also. At other times, the grief was so huge; it seemed like a collective anguish crying itself through me.

Beneath the stone tower at our farmhouse is an underground, vaulted cistern that held rainwater for more than two hundred years. Shortly after my mother died, I emptied this room with Tao, my seven-year-old son, and four friends. Each of us took turns pumping by hand, with an old-fashioned pump borrowed from a neighbor, and then lifted out bucket after bucket of accumulated sludge. We built a simple wooden stairway down into the womblike dark room and shoveled in two tons of gravel for a floor. It was the sacred keening room when our home became the first Shanti Nilaya[10] center in France.

My brother, Bruce, lived across the road and was a devout Zen student at the time. We laugh now when we recall the days when he was earnestly cultivating silence with visiting monks and they would occasionally hear screams emanating from my home.

I envied my brother's silence back then. It took me years to realize that my particular way into the eloquence of silence was through singing, toning, keening, and crying, exploring the vast continuum of vocal possibility. Part of how I grieved was to sing.

---

[10] The name means "final home of peace" and the organization focused on the work of Dr. Elisabeth Kübler-Ross, who wrote *On Death and Dying* in 1970. An extension of Kübler-Ross's Life, Death and Transition workshops, *Shanti Nilaya* offered short and long-term therapeutic sessions for people dealing with the experiences of death and dying.

During my eighteen years in France, I attended more than twelve funerals. Many of the people who lived in the nearby villages were in their eighties and nineties, and they were still shepherding sheep and cows, harvesting grapes, hay, and corn, making wine and cheese, planting vegetables, mending fences, cooking soup every day for their dogs, and living life to the fullest with their families. It was a common occurrence to find three generations living in the same house. My family felt honored to be lovingly received by these unpretentious, earth-loving people. We were the first "foreigners" in the area. Before long, we were helping with the annual harvests, joining our neighbors for meals, and sitting with the shepherds in the long afternoons; and soon we were treated like family.

When we first arrived, there was only one telephone for every three or four hamlets. Our hamlet, Puycalvel, had twelve houses that were built from the ruins of an old chateau that had been destroyed in the Hundred Years' War. My son, Tao, and I would walk through orchards, fields, and vineyards every time I needed to make or receive a call. *Tao* was difficult to pronounce in French, so he was adoringly called Théo, "Le petit prince avec les yeux bleu" (The little prince with the blue eyes.)

Some of our neighbors did not own cars. A bakery truck came once a week, and a small van filled with all sorts of groceries and necessary household items honked punctually at four o'clock every Thursday afternoon. The van was parked beneath a large chestnut tree while many of the Puycalvelians filled their baskets with supplies to last until the following week.

The nearest telephone was in the living room of the Soubira family. Madame Soubira, like many of our neighbors, made her own paté in a large copper cauldron that hung in the open stone fireplace. When Tao was less than two years old, just beginning to learn the names of animals, we went to make a call at the Soubira's house early one evening. A large white duck was hanging by its bright orange feet from a blackened metal hook suspended in the chimney; its blood dripping into a white oval platter nestled into a pile of fresh ashes. *Not* something I had ever seen as a child growing up in California. With pure wonder, Tao pointed to the lifeless bird as he watched the fresh blood dripping from its upside-down beak. In delighted innocence, he exclaimed, "Duckie!"

Life and death were interwoven into a singular piece of latticework among these beautiful earthy people who were part of the landscape and ancient architecture itself. Their way of life embodied the elements of *shibui* that were familiar to me. Not a ripe persimmon in a black lacquer bowl on an elegant bamboo table, but a single sprouted avocado pit in a rusted tin can on an ancient stone stairway, placed with the same kindness and emptiness as any Shinto priest or Zen master.

Shibui à la Française.

I had never seen a rabbit being skinned on a ladder before moving to France. Our closest neighbors, Alfred and Paulette, raised chickens, rabbits, and guinea pigs for food. Sometimes when we walked by their house, Paulette would be skinning a rabbit whose hind paws were nailed to the rung of a broken wooden ladder that leaned against their old stone shed. With exuberance and both hands covered in fresh rabbit blood, she would shout out, "Bonjour, mes cheries!" as she continued pulling off the shiny skin attached to the soft fur. Alfred, hunched with age and nearing ninety, had thick, curly white hair and walked by our house every morning with a wobbly old wooden cart that he filled with wild greens from the roadside.

He and Madame Alibert, who lived ten minutes away, had gone to school together and remembered the days when every hamlet had its own bakery and school. The round bread oven in Puycalvel was in the farmhouse across the road, where my mother lived. Madame Alibert, a few years younger than Alfred, had two front teeth, a frail body crooked with pain, and spent her days in a dark kitchen, joyously cooking meals for her son and making soup for their dogs. Though they owned a small propane stove, she preferred cooking over the open fire as she had done all her life. The white enamel stove was like a relic sitting in the shadowy corner, and Madame Alibert kept her clean dishtowels in the oven and a pile of unread newspapers on the burners.

She loved collecting the chicken and duck eggs from the spacious courtyard, rounding up the sheep in the evenings and darning whatever needed to be mended. Sometimes when we were with her in the barn, she asked Tao to climb over the gunnysacks filled with wheat berries, barley, and rye to find the eggs that she could no longer reach. She walked with a simple, narrow wooden stick, which she also used to maneuver the sheep in and out of their dark stalls. Her husband had died years earlier; and her son, Louis, was a veteran of the Algerian War.

Louis milked the cows punctually after sunrise, and every morning Tao and I walked to the Alibert's farm to get fresh milk, as the sunlight poured across the hills. While Louis strained the warm milk through a small wire sieve, Tao and I visited with Madame Alibert, sharing the ordinary miracles of the moment, day after day. She owned two pairs of shoes, one sweater, two black dresses, and one apron.

Her black sweater was easily as old as I was and must have been mended at least three or four times a year for the past twenty years. She saw no reason to buy a new one.

During the coldest winters, she wrapped her body and legs with newspaper and wore a World War II leather aviator's hat to keep warm. Every spring, she planted purple petunias in tin cans and set them carefully on the large stone slabs on either side of the heavy wooden kitchen door. At ninety-four, Madame Alibert broke her hip and was taken to the local hospital. She begged Louis to bring her home, but the doctors insisted that she stay longer to recover. Louis drove to see her every day in his old pale blue diesel van that smelled like sheep. She refused to eat hospital food, so Louis brought her jars of hot soup and fresh croissants. Two weeks later, she fell to her death from a third-story window in the hospital, trying to escape in the middle of the night. I wept in disbelief when I heard how she died.

One of my dearest friends, Berthe, lived in a village a few miles away. We had met when my son and I were buying a goat. Monsieur Poujade, the man selling the goat, was late, and Berthe saw us sitting by an old stone barn in the shade of an enormous linden tree. As she slowly walked toward us, I could see her eyes glistening. She invited us into her small garden, saying, "There are no accidents, my dear. Mr. Poujade is never late! We were destined to meet." Like most of the old peasant women, she was an herbalist and dressed in black shoes, stockings, a black dress, and a black-and-gray apron speckled with small white flowers. She was deeply connected to the mystery she called *Le Bon Dieu*, and like many of her peers, she rarely attended church. Nature was her cathedral, and the nave was any road that she happened to be limping on. Berthe cooked meals for the local "hermitess" who lived in the hills above her village and was well respected by people in the local community. Berthe loved coming to our home and spending quiet afternoons in the garden. She had never driven a car, so we picked her up in the morning and drove her home in the evening. She delighted in sitting quietly, observing the flowers and birds, sharing lunch with us, and feeling the wind on her skin. It took very little to make her smile with rapture. Every spring Tao and I helped Berthe plant her small garden, and she became like a grandmother that I had never had.

On a small table beneath her bedroom window, she had pictures of her deceased husband and daughter, and there were always fresh flowers brightening the room. Berthe spoke often of Saint Francis and Saint Claire and had a rosary hanging by her simple wooden bed. The morning she died, I could hear the bells from across two valleys, tolling and crying through the mist.

For Berthe, 1978

"Sur cette terre rien est parfait, ma pauvre."
"On this earth nothing is perfect, my poor darling,"
she would say.
She led me through her garden
to show me her lilacs.
Her black apron was torn,
her small hoe tarnished with soil and age.
Cabbage seeds were placed in a row.

"I was paralyzed for ten years,"
she said quietly.
"Now I am seventy-nine.
Warm cabbage leaves
soothe the pain.
Green clay draws the heat."
Her stiffened leg did not bend at the knee.

She carries with her wound a wisdom.
Her gray eyes filled suddenly with tears.
"I lost my beautiful daughter at age eleven,"
her lips trembled.
Her eyes were as the spring in our valley,
overflowing from some hidden source.

Several years before Berthe passed away, Monsieur Soubira died suddenly from heart complications. Like many of our older neighbors, he had been a prisoner of war and was a hero among the region. He had made it very clear that he did *not* want a priest at his funeral. This was unheard of back then. Priests typically gave the last rites whether the person had attended church or not. Hundreds of people arrived in our tiny hamlet to honor Monsieur Soubira, and cars lined two narrow roads halfway down the valley. There were several older men in military uniforms, and some of them carried flags and banners. Madame Soubira could hardly stand. Her daughter and son held her body on either side, like buttresses. After the coffin was lowered into the earth, there was an awkward pause. Without the presence of the local priest, no one was quite sure what to do next. After the initial nervousness, I sensed the most tender and timeless presence, accentuated by the steady hum of bees that had made their hives in the old church walls. Here again was wishlessness, in the very midst of anguish. The silence lasted a long time, and without the need of any ritual or words, everyone simply knew when it was time to throw the flowers and earth into Mr. Soubira's grave. Each mourner came forth, one by one, sobbing or sniffling, moved by an effortless current of blessing. I had picked orange marigolds and bundles of sage from our garden. Tao picked an assortment of wildflowers and made a drawing for Madame Soubira whose delightful, rasping laughter we did not hear for several years after that day. By the time the grave was filled with dirt, the sun was beginning its descent through the branches of oak and the tall green candles of cypress. The bees were still droning when Tao and I walked home through the fields of alfalfa and barley.

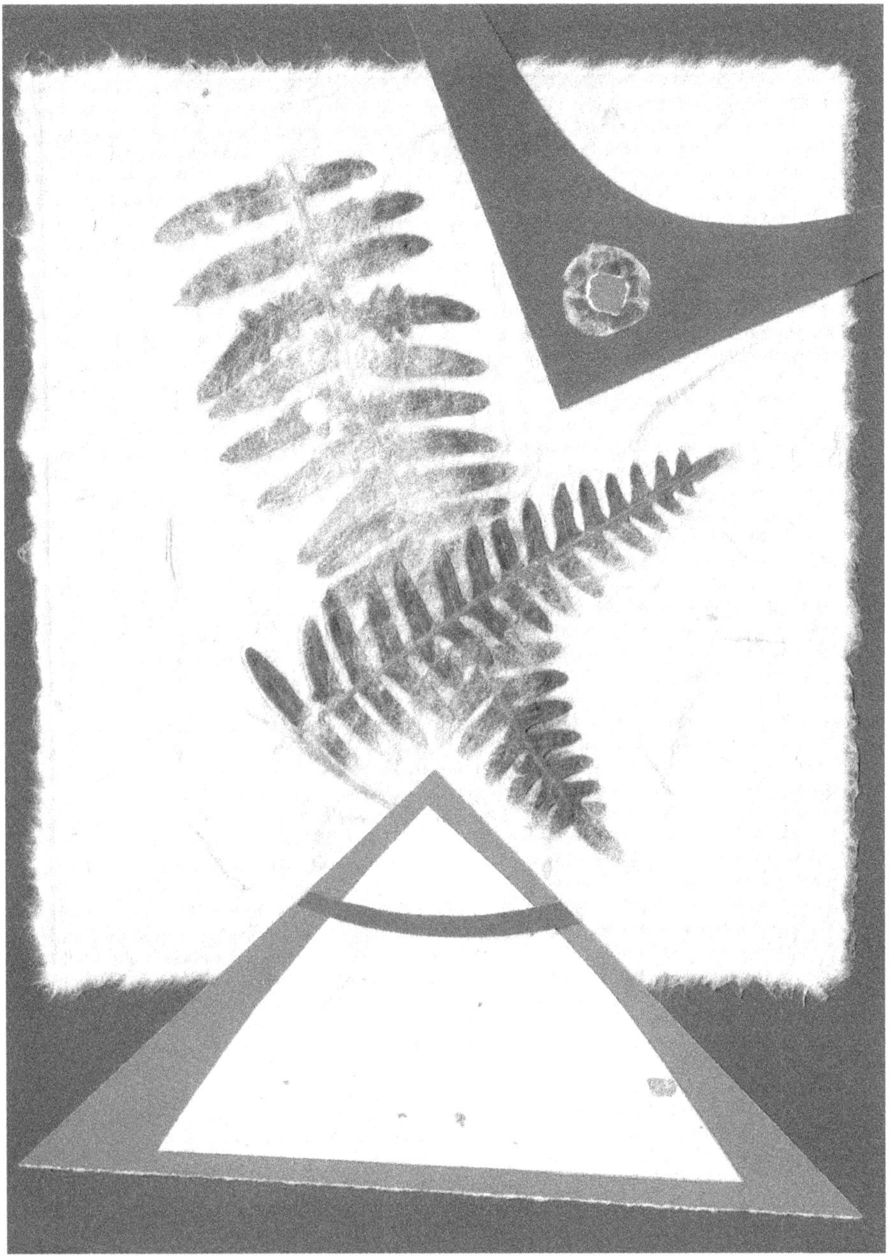

GRIEVING

*We are not broken,
though we have broken open
again and again.*

I am profoundly grateful to the people of Puycalvel and the nearby villages. Their presence with and naturalness around death was an enormous gift. It was in France where both of my parents died and I miscarried my second child. Beneath the old stone tower, in the cool underground darkness, I assisted many people through times of unspeakable grief; and in the open fields and valleys and near waterfalls and abandoned mills, I wept and keened.

There are many ways to grieve. Every person and creature finds her or his own way. Each psyche has its own rhythm and timing. Grief affects everyone differently. I know a man who pulled out his own eye the day after he was asked to identify the corpse of his teenage son. In the Maori tradition, it was customary for mourners to severely cut themselves with sharp shells or stones while singing their lament for deceased loved ones. It's considered a token of their anguish and is still practiced today, though more moderately.

It is easy to become an absolutist in order not to feel the despair that sometimes accompanies loss and anguish. Denial and the longing to transcend pain are part of the grieving process. I have met very few people who are not grieving in some way. Not necessarily from the loss of a loved one, but from the accumulation of a lifetime of losses: the loss of self-respect and disconnection from one's essential nature and the wonderment of life and the myriad losses due to neglect, abuse, and prejudice. These are only a few of the unattended losses buried beneath layers of time that go unnoticed, year after year, and eventually seep like toxic waste into our muscles and sinews, into our joints and bones, and remain for decades like harpoons and bands of armoring. These small losses gradually become like a nest of maggots that eat away at our lives day after day. The sum total of every disappointment, betrayal, broken agreement, every false accusation, and punishment that we received as children; the deeply unconscious loss created as the result of withheld apologies and truths; the loss of one's sovereignty, of friends and lovers and dearly loved pets; losses due to changing schools and homes; the loss of self-dignity due to racism, poverty, homophobia, ageism, and sexism; on and on and on. All of this affects us, somehow, somewhere in our being, in our bodies. *How could it not?* What happens to the repetition of seemingly insignificant circumstances and the overwhelming global situations that we read about in the news and feel whether we read the news or not? All of the above can accumulate and lie dormant, disguised as a sense of hopelessness, despair, and depression. This chronic condition, like a low-grade virus, does not show up in x-rays or blood tests or CAT scans or MRIs. Eventually, after it has moved into our cells and penetrated into our muscles and bones, it is given a name. I remember, in the early seventies, attending a public talk given by Michio Kushi, a macrobiotic doctor. He very gently and matter-of-factly said, "Society is the illness, and cancer is the cure." Those words reverberated throughout my mind for weeks, like a Tibetan singing bowl.

My parents' way to grieve, though I didn't know it at the time, was a kind of alchemy. They took the base metal of anguish and turned it into gold. Their immense suffering was transformed into landscapes of colors and shapes, syncopated by silence and the absence of form. They created paintings, mosaics and poems, gardens and stained glass windows with the healing balm of creativity, direct from the source itself. Over time, I understood the legacy they silently passed on to me. So much of my artwork, for nearly a decade, was inspired by profound anguish. Anguish, interwoven with despair and anger, a potent combination. Enraged by nearly everything, I even criticized myself for being an artist and a singer/songwriter, believing that I was avoiding *real* grief by immersing myself in creativity. I have since come to realize that creativity *and* grief, like all experiences, are openings into that which is inherently awake within each of us, apertures to the wholeness we already are. Creative expression can be a deep form of meditation and prayer. I discovered, also, that there's not a right or wrong way to be who we are.

My parents, who appeared outwardly to be quite different, were complementary aspects of an undividable wholeness. In very different ways, they both showed us through their living and their dying that *something* exists that neither comes nor goes. This realization doesn't necessarily make death or any deep change or loss less painful. It simply becomes a steady overtone throughout the endless encounters with birth and death.

> *This we have now is not imagination.*
> *This is not grief or joy,*
> *not a judging state, an elation,*
> *or a sadness.*
> *Those come and go.*
> *This is the presence that doesn't.*
>
> —Rumi

During the last year and a half of her life, confined to a hospital bed, my mother wrote a twenty-seven-page "creation poem." The following is one of the many stanzas:

> *They took freely from the tree of life*
> *and were alive with gratitude and filled with light*
> *which is not a mystic state,*
> *but simply that of being awake.*
> *Because they were awake*
> *they found that every ordinary day*
> *was paradise.*

A few days before she died, crippled in pain, she wrote,

> *As they lowered me into the coffin to die,*
> *I pulled my knees to my chest like a cricket*
> *and flung myself into the sky.*

Beneath the scattered feelings and the fragments of our past, we are essence, we are wholeness, and we are free. Suddenly, the gate swings wide; the archetype is cast aside, which led us proudly through our lives like a warrior at war. In nakedness we stand, humbled to the core.

Only grace remains.

The earth falls away
on the third of May
so love every moment
of winter.

Yes, back to the poem, this simple poem that was a living koan,[11] and still is. Thirteen years after it was written, my mother died—on the third of May.

The third of May was a weekday. I remember only because my son was at school that day. Bruce and I went to pick him up from the one-room schoolhouse after we left the hospital. Tao and my mother were the best of friends, born one day apart. When he was a year and a half old, he started calling her "Goddi." It was the perfect name for someone whose life was truly hollowed out, hallowed by the deep

---

[11] Used in Zen Buddhism to particularize essential nature, koans are stories, questions or metaphorical narratives that assist one in attaining direct insight and cannot be understood by logic or measured by reason. They take one beyond the boundaries of language and conceptual thought.

estuaries of life. Soon thereafter, many of her friends and family referred to her as this. Even my father called her Goddi, which I found very touching.

Tao was seven years old, and I didn't know how to tell him the news that would indelibly alter his sweet life. We drove to the Vers River and walked over a fallen tree to "Goddi's island," the small island in the river that our mother loved. We had shared many picnics there, and if you sat in just the right spot, you could hear three waterfalls at the same time. It was her favorite place in the valley, and it seemed appropriate to be there when the shattering news was put into words. The local women washed their clothes in the Vers River, and every spring three Gypsy caravans parked in a particular spot, near an old stone bridge. The Gypsies stayed for several months, making willow baskets that they sold in the markets.

I wanted Tao to be told gently and poetically, thinking that this would somehow make it easier to let in. He did *not* want sugar-coated poetry. He wanted the blunt truth. Looking at me with austerity and disbelief, he said plainly, "You mean she's *dead*!" Unable to believe it myself, I simply nodded my head.

There's a place for poetry, and there's a place for the unglamorous truth, even though they sometimes overlap. Give thanks. Tao continues to be one of my greatest teachers. He recently said, "It's not the *poetry* that sucks, Rashani! It's when you veer out of the *reality* of the moment and try to embellish or diminish it in any way." Indeed.

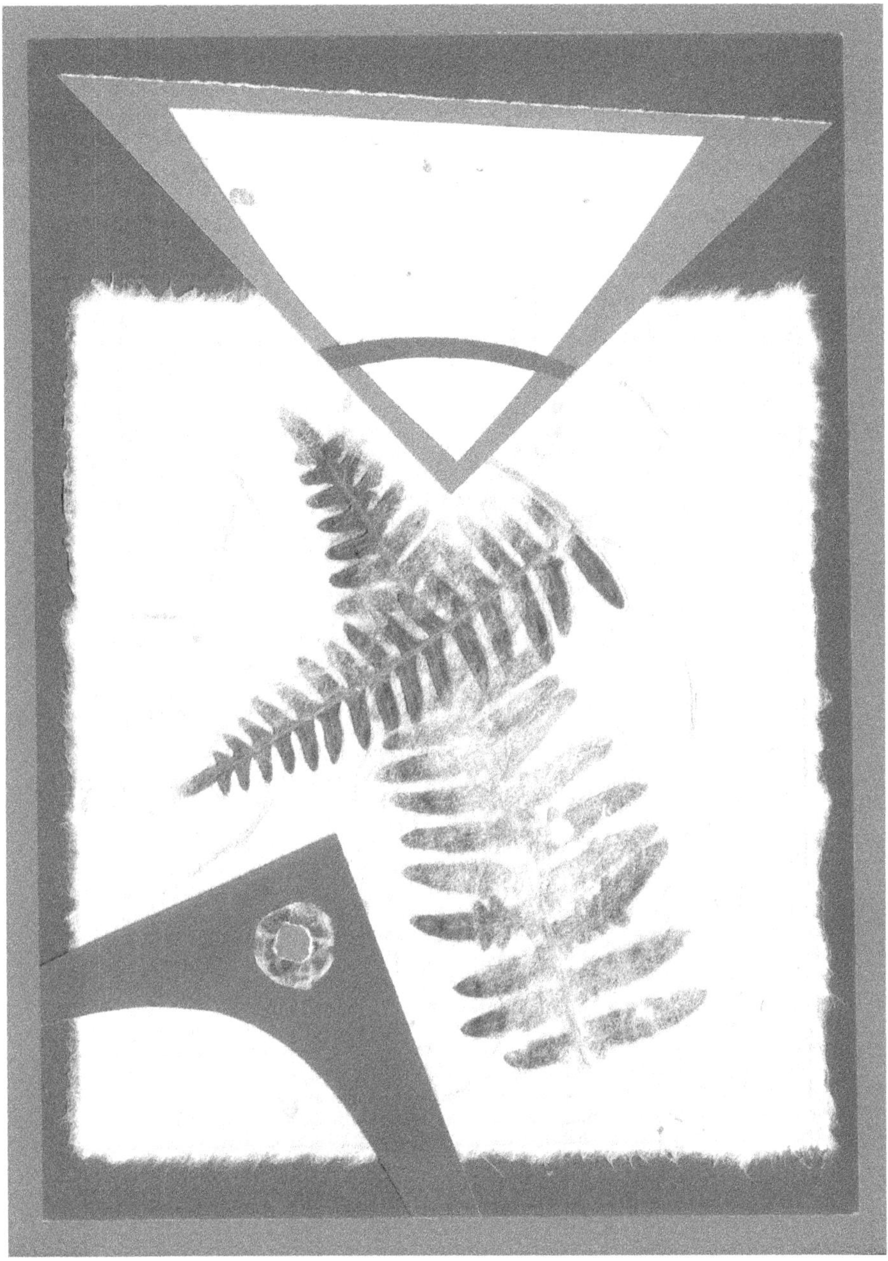

Several years before Goddi died, she carved her own tombstone with a friend. She put it under a tree at the end of her garden and told us that when she died, we could read it. We walked slowly that day to the tree at the end of the garden and found a moss-covered stone nestled in tall grass. Bruce quietly said, "Let's leave the moss." Tao cried out, "No! I want to know what it says." He found a sturdy twig and began scratching away the years of green that covered the carved-out words. When it was finally legible, Bruce read the words aloud, and the three of us burst into laughter. Oh, that glorious humor of hers! The stone reads,

> HOME AGAIN, HOME AGAIN, JIGIDDY JIG

TALONS OF THE DAWN

*Having lost so much
I am beginning to glimpse
what cannot be lost.*

Three months after my mother died, Tao and I traveled to India. I wanted to be immersed in a culture where *everything* was out in the open, where my son and I could experience deathlessness and death in the same breath. I longed to share with him the profane and the divine, not as two separate realms, but as the indivisible tapestry that they are. India seemed like the perfect place. Off we went, hand in hand, in the all-too-familiar aftermath of yet another death. Smack dab into the confluence of all imaginable and unimaginable opposites! Several weeks into the trip, as we walked along a narrow dirt road in a small town in the Himalayas, Tao suddenly blurted out, "It's not *only* sad that Goddi died!" "What do you mean, sweety?" I replied. "Well." After a pause, he continued, "Goddi got to come to India with us, and she didn't need to buy an airplane ticket."

My seven-year-old son was pondering immortality too.

May 3, 2005

*Twenty-three years today
vast wingspan of time ago
I drove to the hospital
earlier than usual,
the converted medieval monastery
in the heart of the Lot countryside
which had been our home
since the early '70s.
I left home
before the sun
had moved over the valley
bleaching like it did most days
the long river of shadows
cast by the tall French poplars.
Your mantra,
that mysterious poem
you had written ten years earlier:
"The earth falls away
on the third of May
so love every moment
of Winter"
had become part of my life.*

*So familiar was that drive
from Puycalvel to Monfaucon.
Every morning
I passed the tenth-century church
opposite the walnut trees
where blackberry vines
tangled in clusters
against the clay roadside
as it curved past the ancient well
where local peasants gathered water
and washed their clothes
in the long, smooth trough.
Then the road descended
into the Vers valley
where once seventeen mills
ground local grains and made walnut oil.*

*When my son was a baby
I took sacks of fresh wheat berries
to one of the mills
and watched the large stones
pulverize the grain
into flour.
I still remember the kindness
and quietude of the old miller
caring for his mother*

who was over a hundred years old,
the way flour dust caught
in the intricate spiderwebs
against the cold stone walls
in the darkened room
and how the chickens and pigs
scratched and pecked and grunted
in the courtyard outside their kitchen.

Then up the hill to Labastide-Murat
whose cobblestone streets
are now covered with asphalt,
along the curving spine between
two valleys, covered with oak and hawthorne
and flocks of sheep.
The small roads
wind through the hills and valleys
joining the small villages
like arteries connecting organs.
The shepherds were the first
to appear in those early mornings,
dressed in dark blue trousers and jackets,
black berets tilted on their balding heads,
locally made wooden clogs
and often a cigarette hanging from their dry lips,
a simple wooden staff in one hand.

*The shepherdesses
carried knitting needles;
balls of handspun yarn
were tucked under their armpits.
With bent heads,
the obedient sheep followed
the monosyllabic commands,
moving like undulating waves of wool
against the ungrouted stone walls.*

*That morning
the wild purple irises
were glowing in their fullness
and the chestnut tree
in the hospital courtyard
had burst into bloom
like flames of song.
Your eyes
though open
were covered with a transparent film,
a membrane of energy
preparing you for death.
Your breath was slow and quiet.
I could not find you
even though your heart
was still beating*

and your gaunt hands
found their way to mine
as I sat beside you
on the starched white sheets
for the last time.
Looking into your eyes
as I had done a million times
disbelief seeped into my being.
"The earth falls away
on the third of May
so love every moment
of Winter."
Here was a moment
impossible to love!
Impossibility wound tight
like a serpent around its prey
until there was simply
silent knowing.
The simple
suchness of the moment
then nothing
and a vastness,
the unknown.
The unknown,
another moment
and the earth began to fall away.

Still looking into your eyes
I quietly asked,
"Can you see anything?"
The child in me wanted to pull you back,
resuscitate you back to life
like she had done with injured rabbits
and baby goats, many years before.
You replied whispering,
"I see your sweetness."
Your last words.
Your sight was no longer
a physical vision.
It emanated from
a deeper realm where matter
decants into spirit
and essence perceives
pure essence.
Equanimity
lured you from the outer
to the inner,
turning your focus
toward the original face
and the current
within the breath
whose love was soon
to disperse you

through the unbreakable
hourlessglass
into everything.
When the doctor forced
the oxygen tubes into your nose
I knew that you were already gone.
When he left the room
my slow hands
as if midwifing a baby into life
prayerfully removed the tubes.

The Photograph
(A journal entry written in 2001)

It was easier to go to India after she died than to stay at home. It took nearly twenty years after her death before I put a photograph of my mother in my room. I am in her arms probably a few months old, and the birthmark slightly off the center of my forehead draws my attention. My mind wanders to India where I remember the colorful caste marks on the foreheads of women dressed in saris. My mother's face is pressed gently against mine. I notice how it's easier to go to India than to look into the eyes of my thirty-five-year-old mother who held me close. What happened to the part of her that went silent amidst the daily insults and the routine of powdered washing detergent forced into her young mouth? She was determined to never insult her children. I notice how it was easier to go to India even though it was there that I saw people with no arms or legs and children with fingerless hands. Open sores infested with flies. Lepers bandaged in unwashed cloth begging for rupees with yellow-green snot draped and hardening on their disappearing noses. Rotting corpses with maggots eating what was once a stomach or face. On our last day in India, my seven-year-old son and I saw a limbless man lying on his back on a narrow rectangular platform attached to four small wheels. With calloused stubs of arms no longer than the width of his face, protruding like overcooked potatoes from his bony shoulders, he was pushing himself along the crowded sidewalks of New Delhi, chanting the names of Sita and Ram, Kali and Krishna. I still remember the uncanny light emanating like visible wind from his clear obsidian eyes. Gently squeezing my son's hand, I whispered, "Don't ever forget this." Two decades later, he hasn't.

My small brown hand touches her freckled arm. My mother is pale compared to my dark skin. In the background is a cottage. Shadows of trees and splotches like quickly made brushstrokes of diluted ink tattoo the white stucco wall. My right cheek presses against my mother's left temple. Her eyes are hidden in the shadow. Her face, though familiar, seems foreign. She is looking into the camera, and I am looking down. If I look long enough into her face, I begin to see my own: the mouth, the chin, even the eyebrows, and eyes. Something else too, which is deeper than the impermanent prayer flag of her flesh. Some part of myself silenced like my mother, even though I never had soap forced into my mouth as a child. Even though I had the choice of washing dishes or writing poetry and was encouraged to find three miracles a day before breakfast with my two older brothers.

Nearing fifty now, I sometimes wonder what was forced into me as a child. Soap at least can be tasted, touched, and seen. Was it the three miracles a day? It's not the miracles I question. I miss what was left unsaid: the explanation of the context from which the miracle practice emerged. Maybe it *was* said. Maybe what I longed to hear was in the reams of poetry she burned the year before she died. Or perhaps it couldn't be spoken. Perhaps it speaks, in hidden equations of color, in the stained glass windows and mosaics that she made during her many hours of solitude. It was easier to go to India and focus on the suffering of others than to feel the calloused stub of my own heart, which pushed day after day for decades against the cracked and well-trodden sidewalks of memory as I continued to chant the names of goddesses and gods.

Talons of the Dawn

Here where the rivers meet
mist gathers colder
than in a dream.
Earth and sky
the song and the cry
are wed and one
between
blurred contours
of mountain and
cloud.

The heart's longing
endowed and deep
like prisms in the
wind
when we scattered
your ashes.

The moon
a golden hawkbell
in talons of the
dawn.

My father died during the full moon. We had spent a beautiful summer together in France, and I returned to New York City by way of London, where Thich Nhat Hanh was speaking about "deathlessness." When I arrived in New York, I received news that my uncle was dying in Ecuador and that my father had fallen and was in a coma in the Toulouse Hospital.

I returned to France the following day. The day he fell, he had spent the morning stretching a canvas for a new painting and was about to teach a class at the home of one of his students. He loved teaching painting and had a handful of avid students in nearby villages.

Katie came to greet him as he drove into her driveway. As he walked toward her, he lost his balance and fell backward. My father remained unconscious for the following two weeks. He was removed from intensive care and taken to a small hospice near Montpellier where my brother lived with his wife and two children. The hospice was in bicycling distance from my brother's home, so we took turns being with our father, day and night.

It was my turn to spend the night at the hospice, and I was thankful for the full moon. Shortly after the sun had set, I heard a crow cawing three times. I had never heard a crow at night before, and it seemed like an imminent knell of a black-winged angel. I thanked her as the last caw was absorbed into moonlight. The crow flew by the window and vanished. I remember singing a song I had learned many years before:

> *Who is in my temple?*
> *Who is in my temple?*
> *All the lights do light themselves,*
> *all the doors do open themselves.*
> *Darkness like a dark bird*
> *flies away, oh flies away.*
>
> —unknown origin

My father had never been to any of my concerts though he loved hearing the cassette I had recorded in French cathedrals and churches. Occasionally I sang for him in the *Saint-Etienne* Cathedral in Cahors where we went shopping every Saturday morning. The double domes created amazing acoustics, and the priest welcomed my songs. We were planning to drive to Scotland the following spring where I was scheduled to perform near the island of Harris, the birthplace of my father's father. As the moon rose higher, above the trees, I realized that this night would be the concert of all concerts.

Nurses came into the room every hour to suction my father's lungs, which were rapidly filling with liquid. When the door opened, I could hear cries from the hallway. Others' loved ones were dying also. Candles were burning in the small room, and I sat by my father's bedside as the death rattle strengthened. The nurses were amazed by the peacefulness in the room and were happy to take refuge in a space of fearlessness and surrender.

Holding my father's hand, I began to sing. I sang throughout the night, till sunrise, and shared songs that I had sung for years but never in the presence of one who was dying. Suddenly they had an entirely new meaning. Three songs wrote themselves through me that night, and I sang them over and over, in between familiar ballads and bhajans,[12] hymns, lullabies, and pieces of Vivaldi's *Gloria* that I had introduced my parents to several years before.

---

[12] A *bhajan* is a type of Indian devotional song, often simple, lyrical, and expressing love for the Divine. The music is based on Indian classical ragas and talas.

I had been a song gatherer since I was twelve years old, and during that precious night, I offered my father every song I could remember.

The following are the three songs[13] that came to me that night:

> *Through the darkness*
> *of this night*
> *and with the fullness*
> *of the moon,*
> *you are returning,*
> *returning home.*
>
> *May the light*
> *of the moon*
> *guide you safely,*
> *may the womb*
> *of the night*
> *hold you gently.*
> *You are returning,*
> *returning home.*
>
> *Death is a gateway*
> *a surrendering*
> *to who you are.*
> *You are returning,*
> *returning home.*

---

[13] Two months after my father died, I recorded an album called *Death Is a Gateway: Songs for the Sacred Passage*. It consists of fifteen of the songs I sang to him.

*Open your wings,
open your wings,
leave the garment
of your body behind.*

*Open your wings,
now open them wide
and be carried
to your destiny
like an eagle
rides the currents
of the sky.
Open your wings.*

Cross over now, beloved one,
to the shore where new life awaits you.
Cross over now, beloved one,
to the shore from whence you came.
There is only love and forgiveness now
and gratitude for all you've given,
there is only love and forgiveness now,
and gratitude for all you've given.

PART TWO

Then there is no miracle,
then there is.

THE UNBROKEN

*We are all alchemists
transmuting pain into aliveness,
unwanted experiences into awakening.*

Introduction to "The Unbroken" by Tom Joyce

"Who's Rashani?" The sheet of paper had been handed to me thirty seconds earlier by Michele Ryan—equal parts transpersonal therapist and spiritual teacher—in her office overlooking the winter green California hills above Tomales. There were only seventeen typewritten lines on the page held between my thumb and forefinger, but the verse had driven a sharp hook directly into my heart. *There is a brokenness,* it began. And by the time my eyes had reached the end, the words were blurred through a veil of tears.

"Tell you the truth," Michele shrugged, "I don't know. Can't even remember where this came from. People send me stuff all the time, and I keep the best of it in a folder. With a name like that, she might be a Sufi." It made sense. The poem had a distinctly feminine quality to it and yet somehow defied gender, transcended even history. It spoke a universal language that bypassed intellect as well. It was a hallmark of the great Sufi poets: Hafiz, Saadi, Khayyam, and, of course Rumi, who had just topped the charts as best-selling poet in America—only seven hundred years after he picked up his pen in Persia. But I'd never heard of Rashani. Neither had Camille Adams Helminski, author of the anthology *Women of Sufism*. "She's not one of the classical authors like Rabi'a al-'Adawiyya," Camille told me, "but maybe a contemporary writer." *Maybe in Iran*, I thought. Maybe Iraq, Syria, Lebanon, Pakistan, Afghanistan, or even Indonesia. A pseudonymous poet whose work would have exposed her to persecution—even execution—a heretic in the finest Sufi tradition, a gadfly to the oppressive Wahhabi and Salafi extremists who seek to purge Islam of nonconformity and universality. Maybe it would be better if Rashani were not exposed, remained an enigmatic crusader opening minds and hearts from beneath the safety of her *hijab* or *burkha*. I let it drop.

Over the next decade, I shared Rashani's verse with perhaps a dozen friends who had reached a crossroad, a moment of openness in which those seventeen lines could bypass their minds and enter their vulnerable hearts. And their reactions were not surprising. Some cried. Some were simply left speechless, simultaneously shattered and renewed, as if they'd had their hearts broken in one moment, then swept up into the gentle arms of their beloved in the next. Reassuring to know it wasn't just me.

Although I abandoned my search for the mystical poet, the poem itself became a catalyst. It prompted me to embrace change, open to possibility, engage in adventure. Those ten years became a time of pilgrimage, an exploration of sacred places, and an inquiry into the nature of sacredness. When I felt it was time to write my own story, put that journey into perspective, I began with a poem—seventeen lines of verse:

> *There is a brokenness out of which comes the unbroken . . .*

"Who's Rashani?" asked an editor with whom I was working. A phantom, I explained. "Well, you can't just reprint someone's poem without permission," she informed me. I told her about my exhaustive and abortive search a decade earlier. "Have you Googled her?" I blinked, stupidly. And that is how I eventually discovered who Rashani Réa is.

Sadly, Michele Ryan didn't live long enough to learn that I'd finally found the mysterious author of "The Unbroken." But I had to laugh at the way I'd imagined Rashani, created her in the image and likeness of a mystical saint, only to find she is very much flesh and blood, very much a woman of this earth. And even though she claimed no formal connection to a traditional *tariqah*, Rashani had apparently been, as the Sufis say, selected as a vehicle for *al-Haqq'*—truth that transcends form.

I wrote to her, mostly to report on what her poem had done to me, never really expecting to hear back from someone with so many irons in the fire of life. I told her,

> *During a very dark time, in which I felt hopeless and lost and in despair, it was as if someone had seen directly into my heart and translated all the pain and love and hope that dwelled inside me—that is me . . . If you wrote nothing else in your life, this one piece would stand as an extraordinary achievement. More than anything I have ever read, it has touched me, spoken to me, spoken for me, inspired and illuminated me. At the risk of crossing the line of skepticism, it has transformed me.*

To my surprise, and delight, that note opened a dialogue resulting in this inadequate introduction to a most remarkable life and, without a doubt, the most extraordinary seventeen lines I've ever read.

"Reason," wrote Jalal al-din Rumi, "is powerless in the expression of love." Forget both your optimism and your skepticism. Leave intellect to its discursive chores and allow this expression of love to penetrate your heart—like a hook attached to a soaring kite.

*There is a brokenness
out of which comes the unbroken,
a shatteredness
out of which blooms the unshatterable.*

*There is a sorrow
beyond all grief which leads to joy
and a fragility
out of whose depths emerges strength.*

*There is a hollow space
too vast for words
through which we pass with each loss,
out of whose darkness
we are sanctioned into being.*

*There is a cry deeper than all sound
whose serrated edges cut the heart
as we break open to the place inside
which is unbreakable and whole,
while learning to sing.*

The Unbroken

Suffering is by no means a prerequisite for anything. It's part of life. We suffer until we understand the root cause of pain. This is simply how the mystery moved through my life and how I have come to perceive it with gratitude and wonder. Your experiences will be different from mine. In truth, we are neither suffering nor free of suffering.

When this poem, "The Unbroken," came to me, I was debilitated with pain and impacted with grief, having lost six family members and several friends. I had just left France, my home of eighteen years, and my sixteen-year-old son had recently gone to live with his father in Canada. While visiting a friend in California, I had a series of blood tests that confirmed advanced Lyme disease. A group of concerned doctors agreed that unless I were to take intravenous antibiotics for at least twelve months, I would most likely have less than a year to live. My immune system was weak; I had little energy, and pain pounded relentlessly throughout my body. I had been in excruciating pain and bedridden off and on for more than ten years, originally from a motorbike accident and later from burning sensations in every joint of my body, interspersed sporadically with chronic fatigue.

Since my son's birth, due to his severe asthma and eczema, I was drawn into the world of natural healing, which I studied in depth. I was particularly drawn to homeopathy and naturopathy, shamanism, sound healing, and dreams. In the spring of 1979, I had a motorbike accident in which I severely ruptured a lumbar disc. After seeing specialists in France, England, and the United States, who all told me that without surgery I would not be able to live without constant pain, I entered more deeply into the world of herbal medicine and quantum healing. One doctor offered me the option of wearing a metal brace for the rest of my life. I thanked the doctors who had caringly diagnosed my injury through CAT scans and x-rays, and guided by dreams and my "hut" (a combination of heart and gut), I sought out shamans and energy healers and eventually received bamboo injections three times a week for the duration of eighteen months. I came to see that part of the gift, from the journey through pain, was the simple recognition of and profound gratitude for the sacredness of the ordinary, the sanctity of day-to-day life, and a reminder of my interdependence with all living beings.

Because Lyme disease was not known in France during the time that I was so ill, none of the doctors I had seen had ever suggested being tested for it. As a result, when what they were looking for in the blood tests showed up as normal,

I was quietly accused of being a hypochondriac. When it was finally diagnosed, I began researching this disease, which is caused from the bite of an infected tick; several friends sent me articles and books, imploring that I realize the seriousness of my condition. Receiving such a blunt prognosis is quite a wake-up call. For many years, while seeing both allopathic doctors and alternative practitioners, I was mystified by the tenacity of the symptoms and astounded that they persisted in spite of everything I did to alleviate them. At a certain point, it occurred to me that what was happening in my body was not *only* an illness, but also a mysterious healing process, a kind of dance or *dreaming*.[14] A rabbi friend had told me that in ancient Hebrew, the word for one who is sick, *choleh*, has its roots in the words "dance" and "dream."

From open-systems theory, I had learned that all living organisms are in a process of self-correction at all times. If this was truly the case, I decided it was time to return to a beginner's mind. I concluded, with excitement, that whatever was happening in my physical body must be something other than only an illness. I was well aware of

---

[14] Not "dreaming" in the Western sense or how it is generally used in the Buddhist context. The *Dreaming* I refer to is a primordial understanding, of the Australian Aborigines, which Arnold Mindell also integrates throughout his work. (See appendix C.)

the severity of the disease and was also drawn to explore the *dreaming* within my untamable symptoms.

From a young age, we are taught to marginalize and pathologize things that we fear or don't understand. For example, Kali, a well-known Hindu goddess, known mostly as the Dark Mother, is seen as a deity of annihilation and embodies some of the most frightening qualities imaginable. Her expression of love is fierce, yet her compassion is no less than that of Quan Yin, the tender goddess of mercy and compassion. In our culture, however, Kali's character is less socially acceptable and deeply misunderstood. So it makes sense that when we discover Kali's traits in our own lives or in others, we sometimes want to automatically repress and pathologize them. Anyone who has watched a child running innocently toward an oncoming car knows this kind of ferocity. It is simply a natural instinct to scream, "Stop!" Kindness has many faces, and I soon discovered that the concept of kindness can be very different from kindness itself.

For example, with fierce compassion, Kali will dismember that which no longer serves truth in order that we may remember our true identity and thus be liberated from all ignorance, falsity, and arrogance. She has been terribly misunderstood and demonized in the West, along with

Seboulisa, Oya, and many other powerful goddesses. It is no wonder that various aspects of these powerful deities appear quite often in women's symptoms and dreams.

Black Mother Goddess,
Seboulisa, Mawu,
Salt dragon of chaos.
Attend me,
hold me in your muscular flowering arms.
Protect me
from throwing any part of myself away.

—Audre Lorde

We are subtly and not so subtly taught to throw many parts of ourselves away, including pain, despair, and grief. How could we not throw parts of ourselves away when we are deeply imprinted by others who are doing the same thing while upholding the pretense of painlessness? Some refer to this as "spiritual fascism."

Seeing symptoms from this somewhat radical perspective, I began to relate differently to the pain in my body. Instead of asking, "What is wrong with me?" I began asking, "What is the gift of this symptom?" "What part of my life is the symptom connecting me to?" "What part of my being actually needs this?" and "How might I need to be more like this particular energy?"

As a child, when I played in the creek for hours and rode my horse in the mountains, I instinctively knew that something much greater than myself was orchestrating the eternal dance of which I was an infinitesimal part. I needed to remember with the same innocent knowing that symptoms were also a mysterious part of the unconditional dance. Being surrounded by an allopathic medical view that is often fear based, it is difficult to remember the dance and the *dreaming*.

I came to understand that symptoms are not merely something to get rid of, but that they are often portals, sometimes labyrinthine, into the fertile garden of our wholeness, an invitation to embrace more of what we are. I noticed how many times a day I was waiting for the future when I would feel better or longing for the past, the time prior to the motorbike accident, when my body was strong and vivacious. I was startled by how much of my time was spent in mental fantasy and how rarely I engaged in simple sensate experiences, in the present moment.

Before the accident, one of my greatest passions was pottery. I was attending a wonderful art school in England and felt elated to discover such a fulfilling vocation. I spent weekends in London and Cornwall, visiting pottery studios and museums, and traveled to Ecuador, where I wrote my thesis on pre-Columbian pottery. After the accident, with a ruptured disc and constant sciatica, I could no longer sit for hours at a potter's wheel, and eventually, it became clear that my *body* was the clay being shaped by the great potter of life itself. It was even too painful to sit on a *zafu*,[15] so I eventually gave up my meditation practice as well. What I discovered, however, was that meditation did not necessarily have to happen in any special place or on a meditation cushion. It was a way of seeing and looking, listening and sensing, and this naked presence could occur anytime, in any place, much like my childhood.

---

[15] A round meditation cushion.

I find that the questions we are asked when ill are limited and discourage any kind of inquiry that allows us to enter into a deeper relationship with what is actually happening in our bodies. Many people automatically ask, "Are you feeling better?" or "Are you better or worse today?" Consequently, we stay in a very immobilized place, restricted once again by the language that shapes our experience.

The mind is so quick to label. It categorizes and interprets, leaving little room for the mystery, the aliveness of the unknown. If we are constantly thinking in terms of *better or worse*, we remain blind to insights that are born from asking different kinds of questions. Implicit in the questions we are usually asked is the assumption that we should be feeling a certain way in order to be healthy, and there's an involuntary disregard of the mysterious life force that is dancing and *dreaming* through us. The right question is like a neurological probe and can take us immediately into the unconditioned mind. "Find the question that will make a difference," one of my teachers used to say.

I discovered that images and concepts were less likely to stay attached when I simply followed the currents of sensation in my body, focusing awareness on whatever was occurring moment to moment. Over time, the questions changed: "Is the part of me that is aware of pain also experiencing pain?" "Who is in pain?" And eventually the questions became "Who am I?" and "*What* is Rashani?" I became deeply curious about this *dreaming* in my body, and my relationship with pain changed completely. The interior galaxy of blood vessels and ligaments, muscles and bones became my meditation hall.

> *Take refuge in your senses, open up to all the small miracles you rushed through.*
>
> —John O'Donohue

Any chronic condition forces us to become more identified with physicality and its wide array of gross and subtle manifestations. Whatever sensations arise, we can simply notice them, and they don't have to be laden with stories, interpretations, or drama. Oh, how the mind loves a good, juicy story. By *story* I don't mean the actual situations that we have experienced, but the conclusions we make that stay with us and shape our perceptions of reality. I'm referring to the stories and beliefs that we cling to for decades that become so deeply ingrained in our thoughts that we rarely question them. These assumptions that become our *life stories* often prevent us from experiencing the reality of the moment and the preciousness of ourselves and those we love.

Over time I began to notice the thin line between bare presence and the slightest exaggeration of what was actually happening. The more I focused on simple sensations, the more I realized that even stillness and inner peace were by-products of something else, unknowable and impossible to name. While deciding whether or not to take intravenous antibiotics, I was reminded of a dream I had shortly after my mother's death:

I was very ill and had traveled with my mother to India to see a renowned woman healer. We traveled for many days to a small village high in the Himalayas, only to be told that the healer had gone into retreat for three years. In desperation, I began to weep. My mother calmly asked if the healer would be willing to heal someone without seeing her. The messenger, a young woman with a shaved head, wearing a brown robe, went to the community and asked. She returned with a pencil and a small piece of paper. Handing them to me she said, "She has agreed to give you a remedy that will cure all of your symptoms. Write your name on this piece of paper and fold it in half." After writing my name and folding the paper in half, I handed the pencil and paper back to the young nun. As she walked away, I shouted out to her my list of symptoms, thinking that I couldn't possibly be healed unless the one giving the remedy knew what the symptoms were! She bowed and gently said, "She doesn't need to know." In that instant, I became utterly calm and was aware of an unprecedented shift happening in my body and mind. The healer was in a tiny hamlet above the community village, and it took quite a while before the nun returned. My mother and I sat in silence, waiting. When the young nun returned, she handed me the same paper on which I had written my name. She said confidently, "This is the remedy for all of your symptoms." Opening the paper I saw, written in pencil and in capital letters, one word:

WORSHIP

It was clear that I had forgotten how to worship life; and in spite of the excellent, professional, and loving advice I was being given, I chose not to take the intravenous antibiotics. If, indeed, I had only one year left to live, I wanted to live it fully, close to the *dreaming* and to be intimate with the ocean and earth.

> *The heart that breaks open can contain the whole universe.*
>
> —Joanna Macy

Synchronistically, I was also called to Arnold Mindell; three different people had mentioned his name to me during the same week. All three had asked, "Are you a student of Arnold Mindell? How you work with people is so similar." I had never heard of Arnold "Arny" Mindell, but it was clear that I needed to seek him out. When I met him, I felt quite shattered and broken open by grief and physical pain. I can still hear Arny's vectorlike words, spoken with great love during our second encounter; "Your most treacherous symptom is your deepest dream trying to happen."

This comment was an unsolvable riddle that changed the course of my life. It seeded itself beyond conceptual comprehension, and though I couldn't explain it to anyone or even to myself, it gave me the courage to trust the unknowable dance/*dreaming* that expressed itself as pain and wisdom throughout my body. Arny's comment disoriented me so profoundly that I gave up trying to understand anything mentally and began to source my whole being while taking refuge in the rare moments of equanimity that appeared like tender saplings in the charnel ground of my cluttered mind. His words ignited a raging fire that burned to shreds anything I tried to grasp with my mind. I knew that there was no way to stop the fire, nor was there anywhere to run or hide. It was definitely time to borrow the beloved's eyes in order to understand that even though my body was depleted and filled with debilitating pain, its wisdom was following a mysterious current of intelligence, a *dreaming* far greater than I could imagine at the time.

So fascinated by this mysterious *dreaming*, which there was little reference to in my own culture, I was drawn to Aotearoa/New Zealand and Australia for eight consecutive years. I spent time with Maori and Australian Aboriginal people and began to see the world through very different eyes. During my last night in Australia, I dreamed that my naked body was painted with earth colors—white, ochre, black, and brown—circles and spirals, dots and carefully drawn lines. I was dancing with a tribe of people who had lived and thrived in the desert for thousands and thousands of years. I was looking into my father's body from the front and from the side, simultaneously. This parallel perspective was evident in the aboriginal art I had seen, but until I experienced it directly, I had no idea of its power. It had the same stripping capacity as a koan, which can instantaneously pull the mind away from the mesmerizing attraction to concepts and effortlessly thrust it through the eye of the duality needle into vast, contentless awareness.

I remember how shocking it was to return to my childhood home in Northern California after living in Europe for several years. The orchards that I played in and rode my horse through as a child and feasted from throughout the summers were gone. Gone! The tall grasses that my friends and I played hide-and-seek in were nowhere to be found. The dusty dirt road that meandered through the apple and apricot trees, where rattlesnakes napped in the hot afternoons, was nowhere in sight. I stood speechless in disbelief.

What I saw instead was a paved asphalt road and a subdivision of houses. "How is this possible?" I wondered. I knew it was happening in many other places, but *this* neighborhood was as sacred as my own body. It *was* my body. The trees that bountifully offered their fruit to dozens of hungry children every summer were our guardians. Their branches taught us about coordination and gravity as we hung upside down, laughing and giggling. The grasses, crickets, frogs and lizards, the rattlesnakes, the wild lupine and poppies that once grew along the edge of the orchard taught us about life and renewal, about the cyclical nature of existence. This once-existing orchard had connected us to the sentient awareness of the earth. The plants and trees, flowers and animals that once lived and breathed here interdependently shaped our lives. The way the moonlight danced through the apple branches in the evenings when I rode my horse home from a long day's adventure was suddenly a memory that would never again happen in this place. The disbelief was riveting. How often do we see clear-cut forests and bulldozed meadows? It has become an everyday occurrence for many people. We have grown so calloused that we hardly notice the rape of our Mother any longer.

I chose not to take the antibiotics and continued listening deeply to the subtlest messages within myself and discovering the connections between symptoms, beliefs, dreams, relationships, and the earth.[16] My symptoms became my teachers and opened me again and again to the parts of myself I had thought I could "throw away."

---

[16] If I had it to do over, I *may* choose to take antibiotics while also exploring the *dreaming*. It is not either/or.

Having spent the past twenty-six years exploring symptoms and their significance in the process of awakening, I have witnessed with reverence the precision of the primordial intelligence of the body-mind. This biostream is millions of years old, continuously evolving, and is inseparable from the earth. In my experience, *every* symptom is a song and cry for wholeness. Rumi said, "The cure for pain is in the pain." Within each symptom is a precise blueprint for the remembering of wholeness. The allopathic perspective[17] focuses mainly on the symptom itself, often neglecting the deeper intelligence that created or *dreamed into being* a particular symptom, or situation, in order for our individual (and collective) being to know itself more fully.[18]

---

[17] By no means do I wish to underestimate the importance of allopathic medicine or create an unnecessary division. *Both* approaches of healing are tremendously valuable and they can work beautifully together.

[18] I am well aware of the environmental factors that are contributing to many, many serious symptoms. Is this a *collective dreaming* of some sort? I honestly don't know.

In order to override the environmental assault on our systems we are impelled to create a larger "body" in which the burden of maintaining our personal and societal health is no longer held in isolation, but can be invigorated through a "field consciousness."

—Emilie Conrad

Is the bowl empty or is it filled with moonlight?

ENDARKENMENT

*Only when my boat
fully capsized in the waves
could I see the pearl.*

This is a circuitous way to get to the poem, yes. Having never been a linear thinker or writer, I am just as intrigued by the creative process, wu wei, and the rheo mode[19] as I was as a child. There is simply a current of energy moving through me, pushing these keys, and creating words. What *is* it? Where do these words come from? Who is writing this book? This energy has an unknowable life of its own. Everything arises

---

[19] *Rheo* means "flow" or "stream." The *rheo mode* is used to refer to the flow of the *dreaming* process.

from and returns to the same sentient awareness. When the sense of doership dissolves, something very simple arises from nowhere. This poem, "The Unbroken," may have been written if none of the above had occurred. I can't really know for sure. All I *do* know is that my life felt like a total mess at the time: broken and shattered.

> *"With the belief in the individual entity/doer, problems never cease. When the illusory nature of the individual is seen, problems never arise."*
>
> —Ramesh Balsekar

My aunt, uncle, and father had recently died within seven months of one another. My father was the last of the three to die, in September. That unforgettable autumn was a colorless molting chamber of transmutation, an invitation to revisit what had felt dismembered through a series of grievous experiences that spanned nearly three decades of my life. This nameless poem, which has touched so many people's lives, came to me like moonlight on a night moth's wing. It was given its title, "The Unbroken," several years later when Estelle Frankel published it in her book, *Sacred Therapy: Jewish Spiritual Teachings on Emotional Healing and Inner Wholeness*.

People continue to ask me, "Where did this poem come from?" I don't know how to answer this question except to say that something happened when I collided with the unknown and found myself beyond all speculation and thinking. Due to my own personal circumstances and for whatever other unknown reasons, my particular journey had included profound anguish and despair. We hear about enlightenment and less about *endarkenment*, which often precedes, and is inseparable from, unconditioned presence.

When my nineteen-year-old brother was asphyxiated, I was twelve years old. Looking back, I see that the shock was so devastating that I could not assimilate it at the time. With each successive death, the trauma layers thickened. Not realizing at the time that my years of singing and keening arose intuitively and spontaneously from the very *true nature* that I thought I was searching for, I continued to seek the absolute for solace. I was in the river, looking for the river, drenched in moonlight, unable to see the moon. Spending time in spiritual communities, for more than twenty years, strengthened my experience of the infinite, yet also deepened my denial of suffering, the invisible tunnel through which I unconsciously disengaged from life.

The broken finger
that once pointed to the moon
was always the moon.

After the sixth death in my family, I felt a shattering throughout my entire being, and suddenly life had little meaning. I had spent time with many people who died and who were dying and had been trained, during my time as an assistant to Dr. Elisabeth Kübler-Ross, to remain calm in the presence of death. Yet suddenly, and quite unexpectedly, calmness was nowhere to be found. Parentlessness was a vast and empty desert. I attempted with great difficulty to metabolize the sudden deaths of my father, aunt, and uncle. I was finding it difficult, perhaps impossible would be more accurate, to locate a reference point for existence. I circled like a wounded falcon in a current of revolving emptiness, unable to feel the wind that I knew was surrounding and holding me. Life's meaning, like a frayed prayer flag, had dissolved.

One night in early December, I was invited to a friend's house, but could not imagine being with even those I loved. My fear was that they would reinforce the montage of who they thought I was, this precarious edifice that was obviously collapsing. I had no words to communicate what was happening. Though it was a great relief to be free from the desire to be someone, apprehension pulsed through my body. Panic alternated with moments of calm inquiry. I watched, with curiosity, the ways in which my ego shuffled the deck of its once-useful strategies, but none of them felt real or worthy of energy.

I wept uncontrollably and was consumed by a fear that I had previously only glimpsed in smaller doses. By midnight, I was not in the abyss, but had become the abyss itself. After walking for several hours, seeing endless epitaphs in the billions of stars that appeared like luminous bullet holes in a black cloth, I kneeled on the cold earth and sang the comforting poem of Thich Nhat Hanh that I had set to music the previous year. It is called "The Song of No Coming and No Going." He had asked me to set it to music before my father died, saying that this is the kind of song we need to sing to our loved ones on their deathbeds. Little did I know that I would be singing it to my father within a year's time.

These eyes are not you,
you are not caught in these eyes.
You are life without boundaries.
You have never been born,
and you have never died,
look at the ocean and sky filled with stars:
manifestations of your wondrous mind.

Since before time you have been free.
Birth and death are only doors
through which we pass,
sacred thresholds on our journey.
Birth and death are a hide-and-seek game.
So laugh with me, hold my hand,
let us say goodbye.
Say goodbye to meet soon again.
We meet today, we will meet tomorrow,
we shall meet at the source every moment.
We meet each other in all forms of life.

I knew the song by heart and had shared it with thousands of people. I had sung it for Vietnamese refugees and watched tears stream from their quiet eyes, as they sat motionless on hand-sewn *zafus* in the *zendo*[20] at Plum Village.[21] I had sung it to American and French Vietnam veterans and their families and had witnessed soldiers weeping for the first time in decades.

---

[20] Meditation hall.
[21] Founded by Thich Nhat Hanh and Bhikkhuni Chan Khong in 1982, Plum Village is a Buddhist meditation center in Southern France, near where I lived.

The deep
emptiness
of saying goodbye becomes the doorway of awakening.

Rashani

What use was it to understand deathlessness while my entire life seemed meaningless? I felt like an impostor, a traitor to my sangha.[22] An abrupt upheaval splintered my thoughts into irretrievable fragments. Sitting on the cold earth, singing the familiar words again and again became blatantly incongruent with my inner experience. This beautiful song that had helped so many people suddenly felt like a false buttress holding up an encrusted structure that needed to collapse. The poetic words I had once loved became shards of a shattered floodgate, void of any relevance. Things that had previously seemed meaningful dissolved into nothingness and were empty of substance. I experienced anger and an aversion to anything that distracted my attention from the unassailable sorrow into which I was being submerged.

Anything other than what was naturally arising, which was the accumulation of more than two and a half decades of exiled anguish, seemed like a useless escape hatch from

---

[22] A community with a common goal, vision, or purpose. A sangha is traditionally referred to "practicing Buddhists," but I like the definition of any group that is devoted to truth. (At the time, I was part of a Buddhist sangha.)

the truth, from the aliveness of the moment. This forsaken part of myself, veiled in shame for so many years, was as tender as any beloved.

The compendium of "I," of persistent thoughts, gave way to silence. The rind of my being, in its habitual striving, dropped quietly. The compulsion to understand or change what was happening disappeared. The many untruths, which had gathered like dust over the years, revealed themselves and vanished as mysteriously as they had appeared. I was being shape-shifted into and by the unknown, pulverized into ash from the curling stem of incense that I had called my life.

There was simply a witnessing of raw experience without rejecting or accepting anything. There was nothing to discharge and nothing to resist. The concept of "I" was melting with an unfolding presence into which the sense of "me" and "mine" quietly disappeared. The content of awareness was suddenly less important than the quality of perceiving, and I realized that the part of me that was aware of pain was *not* experiencing pain. Immersed in open awareness, an undivided seeing suddenly replaced the *someone* who thought she was seeing and feeling.

Something greater than fear, perhaps grace, pulled me deeper and deeper into the epicenter of despair and then pushed me out, farther, into nothingness—and in, deeper, and out and in, then in and out, again and again, until there was no distinction between formlessness and form. It took me past all recognizable edges into the fertile emptiness that I had previously been determined to avoid. Denuded by this nameless presence, I watched the exoskeleton of my entire identity collapse into nothing. Or was it everything?

Where I thought I'd find deep anguish I found instead a portal to God.

Like a flower beyond death,
the world-tree is blossoming.
Two realms returning to oneness.

—Hildegard von Bingen

Endarkenment

The strangest part of that unknowable night was that I no longer held a position against, or for, what was happening. There was no need to change anything. I felt oddly at ease. There was nothing to heal, figure out, explain, let go of, or understand. Anger and grief were nowhere to be found. Even the abyss seemed like another concept. The void was shimmering and had become something other than an object of perception.

I was stillness dancing, yet there was no "I" dancing. There was simply the paradoxical dance of being nothing and everything, the dance of the finite within the infinite, in which we are simultaneously no one and someone. In this collision of "clockocracy" and timelessness, *all* opposites instantly vanished into a seamless entirety.

No longer terrified by the radiant emptiness into which I was disappearing, I picked up a pen and found a small piece of paper in one of the pockets of my well-worn backpack. I honestly don't know how this poem made itself onto the paper. It came through and to me as a gift. The fissures in my heart cracked wider until torrents of love flooded through the broken-open places. While laughing and crying, I realized that so much of what I had previously experienced since my brother's death was an attempt to hide what I had been conditioned to believe was broken.

With the last word scribbled in moonlight, I fell into a dreamless sleep that held me for many hours. When I awoke, the world seemed utterly different and totally the same. I had no words to describe what had happened, only a poem, on a crumpled piece of paper, born of moonlight and tears.

THE POEM'S JOURNEY

*This benediction
moonlight on a night moth's wing,
petals of* prasad.

A few days later, I hand-lettered the poem onto a collage and sent it with several other designs to the card company for whom I was designing cards. The president of the company called me the following week. He was thrilled with the short quotations and was not at all interested in printing the poem. He assured me that very few people would take the time to read such a long poem and that what people want on cards are short quotations, not poems exceeding ten lines.

Something in me protested when he tried to dissuade me from printing it. "I am paying for the printing," I explained, thinking that might appease him. "Even if this poem touches only one human being, it is well worth the money it will cost to print." As I spoke these words, I had no idea what would occur in the years to follow. I simply knew that in spite of his lack of encouragement, I had to trust my guidance. This poem had come as a gift, birthed from the luminous wound sequestered in every being who has known anguish. It was clear to me that it needed to be printed, even if only a handful of the cards sold.

The following year, I began receiving letters of thanks for the poem, then letters and phone calls from people asking permission to publish it in magazines and newsletters. Two musicians wrote to me asking permission to set it to music. Several calligraphers wrote asking if they could handwrite the poem on special papers to make it available for family members and friends. Rachael, a woman from Boston, called saying that she had just been at a large gathering where the poem had been shared. When she asked who the author was, someone told her that Rashani was a thirteenth-century Sufi poet. Another woman in the group laughed and said, "No, she isn't! She's an artist and a gardener who lives in Hawai'i." Rachael and her mother came to visit and ended up staying for a five-day retreat. I was deeply moved that the poem was touching others.

One afternoon, several years later, during the aftermath of another loved one's death, I was alone in my small house in Ka'ū on the Big Island of Hawai'i.

A storm was arriving from the Hilo side of the island, and I was feeling its tremendous energy before the rain began. I remember sitting quietly as a deluge of rain pounded onto the corrugated metal roof. In the middle of this relentless downpour, the phone rang. It was Tian Dayton, a writer in New York City, calling to ask if she could use my poem on the first page of her book that was soon to be published. It is a book called *Heartwounds: The Impact of Unresolved Trauma and Grief upon Relationships*. She said that one of her clients had given her the poem. Tian was one of those unexpected and timely gifts sent by the Mystery. The poem was circling back to me as medicine for my own life.

All of the other books in which the poem has appeared have been as poignantly meaningful as *Heartwounds*. I am grateful for the mutual blessings that have been birthed as a result of this poem.

JOANNA

*What once felt like grief
is the very substance now
of these open wings.*

The following incident occurred in January 2000, on the North Island of Aotearoa (New Zealand).[23] I was a presenter and a participant at a large festival and was invited to offer a seminar on the topic of my choice. I chose to speak about demystifying shamanism and was showing the

---

[23] The Maori name for New Zealand, which literally means "the land of the long white cloud. The use of "Aotearoa" to refer to the whole of New Zealand is a postcolonial usage. Until the twentieth century, Aotearoa was used to refer to the North Island only.

group of about sixty attendees how to connect with the dreambody[24] and how to use symptoms as portals into deeper self-awareness.

The group, roughly half Maori and half Pakeha,[25] joined me near a magnificent Pōhutukawa[26] tree in the garden where the festival was taking place. Several volunteers came one at a time into the center. I guided them by following their movements and explained how we can use symptoms as doorways into nonconceptual wisdom. I had come to discover that symptoms are often expressions of disavowed aspects of our wholeness and was showing people different ways of experiencing fluidity in places where they had known only pain and fixity. Fluidity being the natural expression of the self-healing process that is occurring constantly within us, regardless of what we think is happening. I was fascinated at the time by synesthesia,[27] exploring sensations in places other than where we are being touched, for example, and experiencing the sensation

---

[24] See *Dreambody: The Body's Role in Revealing the Self* and *Working with the Dreaming Body* by Arnold Mindell.
[25] A Maori term for New Zealanders of European ancestry; often used to refer to any non-Maori person.
[26] A coastal evergreen tree, known for its ability to grow in precarious, near-vertical situations.
[27] *Synesthesia* in psychology is the stimulation of one sense alongside another, the evocation of one kind of sense impression when another sense is stimulated.

of taste or smell when a sound is heard or hearing a sound when something visual is perceived.

After several one-on-one interactions, I made myself available for private sessions for the duration of the weekend. As I walked back to the building where I was joining a friend for lunch, a timid-looking woman by the name of Joanna caught my attention and asked if I also worked with psychological pain. "Pain is pain," I replied gently as I noticed her shaking hands. "And," I continued, "like anything else, it can hinder us, or we can use it as a doorway. Often it's an ally in disguise, waiting to be acknowledged." I told Joanna that I would be happy to spend time with her after lunch.

We sat on sun-bleached benches on opposite sides of an old wooden picnic table under an arching tree fern. Her eyes and hands were still shaking, and it seemed likely that it was a drug-induced symptom. This was confirmed when she shared pieces of her journey with me. Joanna had spent several years in and out of mental institutions while attempting to raise a family and finish her doctorate in anthropology. She was under the supervision of two psychiatrists who both insisted that she remain on antipsychotic medication. The medications were worsening her condition, and she found that they blocked her ability to connect with herself and others. Her body looked tired and frail, yet with passion, she shared the teachings of her ancestors. Her grandparents had taught her about *Io*, "the Parentless One who was always existent without beginning or end." [28] She spoke of "being and nothingness," and as she shared stories about her elders, her whole being seemed to

---

[28] The Io tradition among the Maori could be interpreted as a belief of nondualism/monism and similar to the idea described variously as the void, emptiness, or the mind of God. See appendix D.

come alive, and the shaking in her body lessened. "*Io*," she said, "lived since before time in *i te korekore*, the absolute nothingness."

There was more to her sharing than merely a memorized body of knowledge. She had obviously had a direct experience of what she described as "the radiant, hidden face that can never be seen." In listening to her share, I did not experience Joanna to be a psychotic human being. She was present and direct, and I was moved by her openness of being and unhindered clarity. There were no fancy words to describe her experience. It was as ordinary as the tree fern that arched over the picnic table. Emptiness was not some mystifying concept, yet within the psychiatric system, Joanna had no framework in which to realize her own fluency. Beneath her despair and pain was a vastness of heart, her essential being untouched by fear or medication, utterly intact and as lucid as it had always been.

Toward the end of our time together, Joanna reached into her woven handbag and pulled out a faded card. It was one of the five-by-eight postcards on which I had handwritten "The Unbroken" nine years previously. "Are you the Rashani who wrote this poem?" she asked as she carefully smoothed out the creases in the card. In disbelief, my mind remembered the moment when I had defiantly said, "Even if this poem touches only one human being." Stunned, I answered, "Yes, Joanna, I am."

No words could adequately describe that moment of silent recognition. We were two women stripped by loss, who, through beauty and tragedy, had reconnected with the unknowable presence at the heart of all experience. Tears of gratitude quietly spilled from our eyes. The river of tears that carries us home even when we have forgotten where home is, the storyless tears that transform poison into nectar and pain into medicine. As I looked beneath the outer garments of Joanna's wounded identity, I saw a beautiful woman emerging from the labyrinth of her own forgotten radiance.

"I have carried this card with me for the last five years," she said. "This poem kept me alive. When I saw the name Rashani on the list of presenters at this festival, I prayed that it was the same Rashani who had written this poem. I asked for special permission to leave the hospital today so I could meet and thank the person who wrote these words."

Several months later, Joanna called me from Aotearoa. With her doctors' approval, she carefully weaned herself from the medications she had been on when we met. The truth that she had known as a child was more resilient than the medication and the many beliefs that had temporarily convinced her that she was a broken human being.

The moon in any language is always whole.

There are many stories I could share about this poem and have chosen to include only one. I prefer to share a few of the letters and e-mails that I have received to offer a glimpse into how one poem, born of tremendous despair and what felt like death at the time, has the capacity to reach and connect with others. I encourage you, whoever you are, to trust in the essence of your being and to consider that grace is a constant presence, regardless of what is happening in and around you. All paths inevitably return us through the gateless gate to our unfragmentable nature. Masks fall away in the face of love; quills of the past become wings.

Beyond Brokenness
we find what was never lost.
Simply, simply this.

Rashani

SELECTED LETTERS

*In effort's absence
rivers of loving kindness
flow through all beings.*

Dear Rashani,

I'd like to share with you the profound impact one of your poems has had on my life. In January '03, I was diagnosed with breast cancer. A mastectomy, chemotherapy, and radiation treatment followed (coupled with various holistic therapies). I chose to view this difficult path as a transformative opportunity. Even so, it was a time of incredibly intense upheaval: a shattering of body, mind, spirit, and emotions. In the midst of my "dark night of the soul," a friend sent me an unattributed copy of your poem that begins, "There is a brokenness." I was profoundly affected by it and amazed to have found something that so perfectly defined my experience. The poem became my anthem. I kept copies of it scattered around the house and shared it with many friends over that dark spring and summer. On the 11th of October I read it aloud at my end-of-treatment ritual and celebration, by the light of a bonfire on Muir Beach.

It wasn't until just a few days ago that the friend who had found this poem finally ascertained its author. I am so pleased and delighted to have the opportunity to thank you. Your poem served as a hope-filled reminder of the gifts hidden within the suffering. It was an important, pivotal part of my healing, and I truly can't thank you enough. What a wonderful gift you gave us all, making sure it was published!

May you and your work be abundantly blessed,

Barbara Hill

Greetings Rashani,

Your poem found me as I was agonizing over leaving my marriage and changing my young children's lives radically and permanently. The "serrated edges that cut the heart" resonated so much with what I was living at the time. It was clear to me that this poem came directly from within the depths of being utterly immersed in the darkness of unknowing and raw grief, and I was deeply comforted.

Many of us have lost our capacity to "way find" in the dark. We have lost our trust in the dark as the soil of the seeds of life. This poem is like water to our thirsty souls that long to hear once again of the dark and what it can hold for us. I give your poem to many of the people I see here in the cancer program, and the response is universal. A widening of the eyes, tears, an opening of their body as they take it in deeply and breathe more fully. They feel its truth land in their hearts.

"The Unbroken" to me echoes a lost myth in our culture: the myth of the dark as womb of the light. So much focus on the *light* ... of consciousness, of a luminous deity, of understanding and so little about being in the unknown, in darkness. This is what resonates so very deeply in my bones. My bones remember and hunger for the truth that the darkness of human experience is the very soil from which life emerges. For me your poem births genuine insight in a way that honors the anguish from which it is born. Such insight, clothed in flesh, blood, and tears, can sustain the human soul through the most terrible suffering. This is a rare, rare thing in our age of quick and cheap hope concretized in religious ideals, material goods, war, addictions, and so on.

The journey from which this poem was born reminds me of the ancient myth of Persephone and Demeter. This myth speaks of the significance of recognizing that dark and light are not opposing forces but entwined deeply in the spiral of life. This is an awareness some of the people I journey with through cancer find themselves thrust into discovering.

In the myth, Persephone was seized from Demeter's arms, her mother, in the bloom of summer and dragged into the realm of death where she was forced to become its queen. This is often how the experiences of illness and grief feel to us. Like Persephone, we are no longer the innocent daughters of the summer land. Persephone also, by unwittingly eating six pomegranate seeds from the lord of the underworld's table, had to forever assimilate dark and light, summer and winter, and was initiated into her womanhood through her journey.

Through griefs not asked for, you too were forced into the watery underworld of tears and pain and uttered what came through to you from this journey. You speak from within this darkness, with the six pomegranate seeds of loss and death, assimilated, digested, and forever a part of your cells. The poem speaks of the loss of connection with life and the emergence of a deeper connection to the unquenchable life source that returns summer to the land yearly out of the womb of darkness.

It is rare for gifts of the underworld to be claimed successfully. This poem is one such gift, revealing a possibility of what our own journeys through the underworlds of grief, loss, injustice, rage, whatever our particular sorrow might yield if we stay the course, live into the anguish, and trust the dark. By letting go of the light, we allow ourselves to be drawn into the sacred womb of darkness where we can gestate in the unknown and be reborn into a new song.

"The Unbroken" pierced through the dark night in your life and carried you lovingly through the unknown, into the wholeness that had been within you all along. This poem and that which brought it into being shows us that such a possibility exists for us. How this experience comes, we can never know; but that it can come through the deep breaking open of our hearts, we are encouraged by your poem's very existence and its incredible journey around the world, to trust.

You have gifted us with the deeply comforting truth that our essential nature, no matter how shattered we may feel, is whole and unbreakable.

Thank you for your gift to the earth community through your work. Your deep commitment to nonduality and presence continues to ripple through many lives.

Helen

Helen Battler, MDiv
Specialist in Spiritual Care
London Regional Cancer Program

Hello,

I am Jennifer Martin, a freelance writer living in San Antonio, Texas. I am currently self-publishing a book, *Star Child: A Mother's Journey Through Grief*. When I first read your poem, "Twhere is a brokenness," I knew two things: great sorrow had touched your life, and I knew I had to find a way to include your writing in my book.

Every line in your poem tells my story and the story of any other parent who has lost a child. The death of a child is that "brokenness, that shatteredness, that hollow space too vast for words, and that sorrow beyond all grief," which you write of so poignantly.

But most important is that through the rite of passage we know as death, we are, as you exquisitely say, "sanctioned into being"; and when grace envelopes us, we can "learn to sing" again.

Grieving my son's death sanctioned me into being. The sorrow and brokenness that shattered my spirit and my heart was unfathomable. Several years following my son's death, one morning, at dawn, I found grace in a rain-washed morning sky, felt the presence of angels and the spirit of my son, and I was somehow made whole again. The day I found and read "The Unbroken," that same feeling engulfed me; grace enveloped me as I wept.

In gratitude,

Jennifer J. Martin

Dear Rashani,

"The Unbroken" represents for me the possibility inherent within the suffering of grief, that when suffering is perceived as a sacred wound, there is potential for transformation. I am currently completing a clinical case study, entitled "The Initiatory Potential of Grieving the Loss of a Loved One," for a doctoral degree in clinical psycholog and would very much like to use your poem.

I often read your poem to group participants to give them hope that they can endure their suffering and, in the process, gain more understanding of themselves and life in general. Your poem always brings tears to my eyes and to those I read it to because it is so moving and genuine and true. I experienced the deaths of my first husband, mother, and grandmother within short order about ten years ago; and the fist time I heard your poem, I felt held and soothed and knew that all was well with the world.

Warm wishes,

Ilke de Gast

Hello.

I am a Sister of Mercy in Philadelphia who is preparing an article in our community in-house publication. I would like to include your exquisite poem "There is brokenness." Thank you so much for your consideration. Our community is going through change that will require courage and consolation. I believe your poem will help us to touch brokenness more deeply. Your words seemed the perfect conclusion to the attached article. Let's keep one another in prayer and hope. May the blessing you offer so generously give you joy and continue to offer healing in the universe.

Sincerely,

Sister Maria DiBello, RSM

P.S.

I was given your poem when my youngest brother took his life. It was a source of immense comfort to me. I am not surprised that God offered it to you after such grievous losses.

Dear Rashani,

I have been deliberating whether I should send this e-mail or not. It's not usually the kind of thing I do, but somehow I feel I must share the effect your words have had upon me.

I have been anorexic for over twenty years. I have also had problems with self-injury, drug and alcohol abuse, and depression. I have been in and out of hospital and have overdosed numerous times. This behavior stems from an abusive childhood, I believe, which lasted well into my teenage years. I have been pronounced by many doctors and psychiatrists as "a lifer" or incurable.

In 2001 I ran away from my life in England. I was tired of fighting something I couldn't see. I was tired of trying to be something I wasn't. I packed two suitcases and boarded a plane with $300. Anyway, to cut a long story short, in October of 2001, I found a book that had some of your words written in pencil in the front. The poem begins:

> There is a brokenness
> out of which comes the unbroken,
> a shatteredness
> out of which blooms the unshatterable.

These words have become my mantra. My slogan. My life. They were a light, a hand of divine inspiration reaching out to lift me up in those dark, lonely days. I have become one of the unbroken. I have healed from a laundry list of psychiatric problems so long that some psychiatrists simply didn't believe I was functional. I no longer harm my body in the pursuit of silence, of wholeness, of self-preservation.

Thank you for sharing your beautiful words.

Love, blessings, and peace,

Willow

Dear Rashani,

I love your poem and share it frequently. On most retreats these days, I read it to the group at least once, often as the close to a talk, particularly one talk I give on the judging mind. Self-judgment is such a prevalent experience for most people and learning to have genuine *metta* for oneself is the key, I believe, to an awakened heart. I find your poem beautifully articulates just what I want to convey to practitioners, that underneath all the hindrances, confusion, and pain lies a Buddha. All the wisdom and love we could ever imagine is right inside waiting to be discovered or remembered. When I read it to a group, invariably people request a copy or ask me to post it on the board. It has touched many people in their most open and receptive state and, I think, has been a pointing-out teaching for them to see the truth of their Buddha nature.

Thank you for writing such a beautiful piece. Thank you for being such a clear channel that allowed it to come through.

Much *metta*,
James Baraz
Spirit Rock Meditation Center

I am writing to contact the artist Rashani.

My name is Deborah Massell, and I am in the midst of writing a dissertation on the early twentieth-century French composer Lili Boulanger for the University of Montreal in Canada. My request is to have permission to use one of your beautiful poems as the opening quote for my entire dissertation:

> There is a brokenness
> out of which comes the unbroken . . .

My mother gave me this poem years ago typed up on a piece of paper, and I never knew how it came to be. I looked you up online recently and found this poem on one of your note cards. The images and the feelings for me signify the depth of pain out of which comes the artistic creation, and for the composer Lili Boulanger, it is like a mirror reflection of her brief and tragic life.

Here is the very beginning of my dissertation:

There is a brokenness... (It begins with the poem.)

The above poem, with its unusual, beautiful, and seemingly contradictory images, may be said to symbolize the spirit of Lili Boulanger. We are dealing here with a woman who suffered enormous physical trauma throughout her brief and tragic life, yet was able to distill every moment into an act of pure creation, one that transcended the tragedy of her condition; she became like the water lily itself: an exquisite flower which grows only out of the deep mud of the lake, a perfume of joy and beauty created from a swamp of darkness and pain. In her music she managed to combine these two elements of darkness and light, agony and joy, hopelessness and inspiration. Indeed, her whole abbreviated life and her extraordinary struggle to live and create in spite of overwhelming odds, reflects this essential duality.

Your poem is truly a miracle in itself; and I know my mother, Sylvia Perera, has loved it and, as I said, felt a kinship with its spirit for years as well. I am including her in this e-mail exchange because she will be joyful to read your greeting and to know more about the poem's origin.

Again, heartfelt thanks, and enjoy the summer.

Deborah

Deborah Massell,
Lecturer of Voice
The Crane School of Music
Potsdam, NY 13676

Dearest Rashani,

I am writing because I feel I must share the synchronicity that led me to you and to thank you for your poem, whose song and vibration continue to sing and bring peace to my soul.

Why is it that so often, we, as a collective, do not acknowledge the sacred teachings of the wisdom bringers until long after their physical form has moved on? And how fortunate are those, such as myself, whose lives have been touched and forever transformed by having stumbled upon a single poem arriving serendipitously by a living awakened one and all at once feeling seen and understood while standing naked in the deep dark abyss: vulnerable, shivering, lost, and alone.

On October 8, 2007, my son fell forty feet from a cliff and lay there for quite some time, yelling, until a housekeeper heard and found him. His back and both legs were broken. The haunting cry of the banshee arose from deep within my chest as my knees buckled, and I crashed hard to the floor. A mother's grief knows no boundaries, has no decorum, and holds back no release. The wail rose and filled the house, its vibration soaring and swirling out into the mist, cutting a path into the ethers where it met and connected with the vortex of grief now circling this planet, a grumbling, rumbling veil of tears. Spent, my head dropped to my knees, and my body curled to cocoon my heart. The veil was breaking. The world went black on that day.

From that day forward, the life I had made began to fall apart. Nothing in my life seemed to make sense anymore. This time, my path was not toward the light. This journey is chthonic, actually a descent into the underworld. I began to discover ways of being that felt more alive and authentic to my soul, all the while knowing I would soon need to find a quiet space away from all the hustle and bustle to release the unfinished grieving I had stored away. It was then that I happened upon a kindred spirit who would prove to be the leading domino in a trail of connections that would eventually point me in the direction of my awakening.

Drawn by the vibrancy of a young woman at a Dance for Universal Peace event, I decided to ask her to what she attributed her obvious joy. She told me of a woman named Rashani whom she had met while at a retreat in Hawai'i, whose very presence, for her, had been life-changing. She spoke of serenity, nonjudging wisdom, deep listening, and a woman who had walked an incredible life path herself and who had gained much empathy in the process. I knew when I got home I would Google this woman, Rashani, who had touched my new friend's life profoundly. Signing on to the Internet, I opened Rashani's Retreats and came upon a poem that immediately unleashed the floodgate of all the grieving I had tucked away so carefully.

I read the first line, "There is a brokenness out of which comes the unbroken" and felt an immediate connection from deep within me. It was as if a tiny musical thread had slithered in and was dancing around my heavy heart. As I continued, "there is a sorrow beyond all grief, which leads to joy," I then felt someone pluck that string, and music began to fill all the hollow, empty spaces. But it wasn't until I read the words "out of whose darkness we are sanctioned into being" that I knew I was no longer alone. I knew someone, this Rashani, was there with me in the darkness. Tears rushed like a monsoon down my cheeks and splattered over the keyboard. And when I read "There is a cry deeper than all sound whose serrated edges cut the heart," I viscerally felt the words vibrate down the length of that musical thread, cutting at all the veils I had wrapped around my heart over the years, making it shudder and shake in its new aliveness in my chest.

This poem became my song of hope, a song of connection, of being heard; and its music and vibration are forever one with my healing heart. "As we break open to the place inside which is unbreakable and whole." With each reading of your poem, I feel light vibrating down that thread allowing me to see in the darkness the place inside which is whole and yes, Rashani . . . I *have* begun to sing. The block I had, is removed, and I now have a *voice*!

Bless you for being not only a vanguard but for being a conduit of the healing energies housed in the creativity of the *now*.

Forever grateful,

Christine Hendrix
Instructor, Skagit Valley College
Washington

Dear Rashani,

Greetings. My name is Jarem Sawatsky. I teach peace and conflict transformation studies at the Canadian Mennonite University in Winnipeg.

For the past five years I have used your beautiful poem, "The Unbroken," to start my Intro to Peace and Conflict Transformation Studies class. It captures so well so many aspects of the pain and potential of life, conflict, and, I think, also peace and justice. Thank you for this wonderful gift.

For the past three years, I have been working at my doctoral research—a comparative study of three communities that have some practice of healing justice. I hung out at three communities that agreed to participate in this study so that I could learn as much as possible about what healing justice is, how they practice it, and what they believe is necessary to sustain a more healing way of justice. The communities include Hollow Water, an aboriginal and Métis community in Canada; the Iona Community, an ecumenical Christian community based in Scotland; and Plum Village, Thich Nhat Hanh's Vietnamese-initiated community in Southern France. What a treat.

I am publishing my research with Jessica Kingsley Publishers (UK), entitled *The Ethic of Traditional Communities and the Spirit of Healing Justice: Studies from Hollow Water, the Iona Community, and Plum Village.* I would very much like my opening introductory chapter to start with your poem "The Unbroken." I use the poem to introduce the idea that perhaps justice does not need to be all about pain and punishment. Directly after your poem, I ask the following questions: What if justice is about becoming whole while learning to sing? How do we nurture the conditions where shatteredness might bloom into the unshatterable? What imagination and support is necessary to sustain that journey into darkness where we are sanctified into being? How do we cultivate the ability to hear the cry that is deeper than all sound and to see the unbreakable in the broken? What if justice is meant to lead to joy, to emerging strengthened out of fragility, to finding our place in the song? What if many of our basic assumptions about justice are misguided? What if a more healing kind of justice is possible? What if it already exists?

Once again thank you for the gift of your poem. It continues to have impacts beyond your knowing.

Take care,

Jarem Sawatsky

Rashani,

"The Unbroken" describes my life, in a nutshell. It describes my experience of being cast into an unbearable amount of suffering, several times in my life, only to emerge as a new being. In my work as a researcher, I focus on the topic of humiliation. I have had experiences of utter humiliation in my life, so deep that they almost erased me as a human being, socially, psychologically, and almost physically. I would never have thought that there would be a time in my life where I would *sing*, where my entire life would have turned into a song or, as I perceive it, a *wave* with no anchoring, a wave of humility and love.

Your poem, in its last line "while learning to sing," so graciously captures the almost unimaginable experience of fluidity, the pleasure of refraining from clinging to fixities, the delight of floating in flux. This song means *life* despite the fear of getting lost, of falling into a void. Your poem paints the entire spectrum from utter despair to utter liberation, liberation even from liberation.

In loving appreciation,

Evelin G. Lindner, MD, PhD, Social Scientist

Dear Rashani,

I am writing to ask permission to sing a setting I have composed of your poem "There is a brokenness." I would like to sing the song initially in a concert on the twenty-seventh of July and am sure I will like to sing it again thereafter. I have only just discovered that the author is twenty-first-century and not a thirteenth-century Sufi as I was led to believe, hence the late request!

It is going to be sung in a very beautiful space in a foyer with a huge glass window and balconies and a wooden floor in the Covent Garden Royal Opera House in London by an amateur choir of about fifty-five and boosted by some soloists I sing with.

I would like to send you some of my recordings and will put some in the post. Eventually I would love to record your song for an album too but am not yet ready. I will certainly send you a rough copy from the concert.

I send you all good wishes,

Helen Chadwick

Hullo Rashani

I am a member of the choir that recently sang your poem "The Unbroken" in the Royal Opera House in London. I wonder whether you practised Zen meditation with Aitken Roshi, who is, or used to be, a Zen teacher in Hawai'i connected to the Zen group of which I am a member—the Sanbo Kyodan, based in Kamakura, Japan, but with sub groups in the US, Europe, Southeast Asia and Britain.

I thought I recognized something (nothing) in your song and that perhaps we shared a common experience. I practiced Zen in Japan with Yamada Koun Roshi during the late '70's till '81. Like you, I have tried a variety of things, even spending nearly two years in a Zen monastery in Japan—very tough. The monastery—Ryutakuji (founded by Hakuin) is famous for, among other things, a collection of classic Japanese paintings, which are exhibited for one day each year in late November. One of those paintings has the words "No birth, no life, no death," inscribed upon it. For me, while lots of other things can help, it's the direct experiences of "No birth, no life, no death," which really do the trick—"a hollow space too vast for words" as you have so aptly put it. Needless to say, I still practice Zen. And, needless to say, I enjoyed singing your song very much. In fact, at times I felt so moved by it that it was difficult to keep on singing. Fortunately, being in a choir all I needed to do was keep opening and closing my mouth like a goldfish, so nobody noticed my sounds of the soundless were all too literally soundless.

I look forward to meeting you some time,

Ian

Rashani,

Attached is a low-resolution PDF of my song setting of "The Unbroken."

About 3 years ago, at a time when I was concerned about my ego taking over in composing music, I had an interview with the teacher at Zen Center Los Angeles. She said something like: "If you want to write the world's best piece of music, go ahead and do it. After all, it is your offering." It took at least a couple of years of resisting that message for me to begin to see what she meant. Working on setting your poem has been a catalyst...

With appreciation for your poem and the practice it points to,

Justin Weaver

AFTERWORD

There is only love.
All else, repeating stories
exhausting themselves.

Though it was not my intention to write a memoir, this book shaped itself as I surrendered, day after day, to what was being written. The first few sections appeared after I thought the book was finished. For the past five years, I have been exploring the difference between doing, not doing, and nondoing. Nondoing is simply a response (or a presponse)[29]—neither active nor passive—to what is occurring in any given moment. Each morning, as I sat down to write, I would not begin writing until the desire to say something had disappeared. It was a fascinating exercise in "nonwriting."

---

[29] See appendix F.

After months of writing, I edited out more than a hundred pages and thought the book was finished. Three friends urged me to put the edited parts back in. I kept asking, "What does my childhood, the study of symptoms, and my years in France have to do with this poem?"

As the words continued to pour through, describing what I thought was the past, I quietly realized that there is no past and that what I am writing about exists right here, right now, co-arising from the unbroken reality that prevails prior to any memories and is present with every breath, with the beating of this heart, the blooming ginger in my garden, and the singing of birds. It is free of memory and abides in the unknown.

Several friends encouraged me to share about my childhood. "That way," insisted a close friend, "your readers will know that you were just as neurotic and as infinite as everyone else and that no one need be a thirteenth-century Sufi or a mystic in order to realize their true nature!"

I laughed.

An acquaintance called the other day in an exhausted state, having taken on too many projects and jokingly exclaimed, "I sure hope this poem is true!" Is the sky true? Is the ocean true? Is love true? "The Unbroken" speaks directly from the relative and the absolute, celebrating the inseparability of our ordinary humanness and the essential nature of being.

I remain in wonder as to how this poem birthed itself and how it continues to have a life of its own that deeply touches people. It finds its way into others' lives as mysteriously as it found its way into my own. Anguish and grief often remove the last vestiges of our identities in order to reveal the essential, interdependent nature of who we are. I recognize the process of breaking open as an aspect of the human condition that, when entered fully, has the capacity to liberate us from the despair of suffering. Paradoxical as it may seem. Regardless of our age, social status, gender, color, religion, or beliefs, we all encounter life's impermanence sooner or later. That annihilating inoculation of holy aloneness stops us in our tracks. All paths disappear in this startling visitation, and the illusion of security is replaced by a vast groundlessness through which we have the opportunity to become servants of the compassionate, broken-open heart.

Every time I receive a letter about this poem, I'm reminded that as all sorrows collectively ripen, we are grieving and awakening together, not in isolation. We are invited, again and again, through every experience—whether it be blissful, neutral, or painful—to remember and celebrate the sacred web of life. I hope that reading these letters and having a small glimpse into my life's journey allows you to feel the presence of others and shows, in some small way, how interconnected we all are. In the vulnerable dialogues that occur as a result of anguish, we often become connected more deeply than before. Our different passages through painful and challenging times are not without gifts that come to us unexpectedly.

The experience of wishlessness that I first discovered and delighted in as a child is the presence that remains. It is not a transient state, nor is it dependant on inner or outer circumstances. It is the actual condition of experience itself before any effort is made to change it. I love this word, wishlessness. There's something about the word or the way it was spoken or maybe the way the wind was blowing when I first heard it. It captures, for me, the primordial, sentient essence of every being and is similar to the Australian aboriginal understanding of dreaming. This unconditioned presence is not the result of any particular cause and does not disappear in the absence of a given sensation or situation. We are all born not with but as this. It is what we are beneath our many identities and is not something we need to achieve or acquire or are blessed with as a result of gaining merit, nor can it be taken away from us as punishment. Wishlessness, intrinsic awareness, innocent wholeness, Self, unconditioned presence, original face, true nature, whatever we choose to call it, remains untouched and unbroken amidst that which appears and disappears and is changeless.

Afterword

A few years ago, I returned once again to my first home in Northern California to discover something very unexpected. This time, as I entered the neighborhood that had been the magical garden of my childhood, I could feel the dreaming of the apple trees and blue belly lizards, the dreaming of the poppies and lupine and of the ripe apricots that fell to the ground when we shook the trees more than four decades earlier. An aboriginal friend had said to me, "You can kill a tree, but you can not kill the tree dreaming." I realized that the orchard, though visibly gone, still existed beneath, within, through, and all around the asphalt road, driveways, and houses. Indeed, not even the developers could take its essence away. The sentient essence of apple blossoms and all of the myriad species that once filled the orchard still existed in the dreaming. Even the apple tree, the rattlesnake, and the blue belly lizard have an original face.

Perhaps this was the same "miracle of orchard breath" that had thrust itself into the face of Edna St. Vincent Millay.

Rumi said,

> Learn the alchemy true human beings know:
> The moment you accept what troubles you've been given,
> the door will open.
> Welcome difficulty as a familiar comrade.
> Joke with torment brought by the Friend.
> Sorrows are the rags of old clothes and jackets

> that serve to cover, then are taken off.
> That undressing, and the beautiful, naked body
> underneath,
> is the sweetness that comes after grief.
> The hurt you embrace becomes joy.
> Call it to your arms where it can change.

In the "undressing," alchemy simply happens in the flames and fluidity of life, which are constantly moving and dreaming through us. We are fluid organisms in a resonant field of energy, a verb more than a noun, an ever-changing process, and a candle flame more than a candle.

It is not a matter of banishing grief but turning toward it with tenderness, opening to whatever it will reveal. By "calling it to our arms where it can change," we discover a deeper aspect of joy. Joy is not the removal of grief, but the capacity to meet whatever arises moment to moment with compassion. Can we trust our brokenness enough to look and feel deeply into its sentient essence?

Through the crucible of anguish, we are often forced into the unknown, where we enter like a caterpillar, the process of liquefaction. This is a total melting, similar to the creation of glass. The raw materials must be heated to extremely high temperatures in order to become liquid. As the liquid glass expands, form and empty space are created in the same breath. It is here, at the interface of death and deathlessness, that we begin to sing!

Voila! And then, just when we think we've arrived, we discover that the nature of being is a constant, lifelong letting go and wearing away of anything that is not essential. And the erosion continues, moment by moment, day after day, for the rest of our miraculous, ordinary lives.

In the spirit of the sweetness that comes after grief and the haunting cries that occur before we taste the sweetness, I thank all of you who took the time to write to me, including the many whose letters and e-mails are not included here. And to those whose suffering has yet to reveal the wholeness and belovedness of your being, I offer this book as a gift of love.

Rashani Réa
Esmeraldas, Ecuador.
June first, 2008

APPENDICES

APPENDIX A

"The Unbroken" has been published in the following books:

Heartwounds: The Impact of Unresolved Trauma and Grief upon Relationships by Tian Dayton (Health Communications, 1997)

Sacred Voices: Essential Women's Wisdom Through the Ages by Mary Ford-Grabowsky (Harper San Francisco, 2002)

Silver Linings: The Power of Trauma to Transform Your Life by Melissa West (Fair Winds Press, 2003)

Sacred Therapy: Jewish Spiritual Teachings on Emotional Healing and Inner Wholeness by Estelle Frankel (Shambhala Publications, 2003)

Woman Prayers by Mary Ford-Grabowsky (Harper San Francisco, 2003)

Stations of Light by Mary Ford-Grabowsky (Doubleday, 2005)

Starchild: A Mother's Journey Through Grief by Jennifer J. Martin (iUniverse Books, 2006)

Untrain Your Parrot by Elizabeth Hamilton (Shambhala Publications, 2007)

The Way of Mary: Following Her Footsteps Toward God by Mary Ford-Grabowsky (Paraclete Press, 2007)

The Ethic of Traditional Communities and the Spirit of Healing Justice: Studies from Hollow Water, the Iona Community, and Plum Village by Jarem Sawatsky (Jessica Kingsley Publishers, 2008)

The Power of a Broken-open Heart: Life-Affirming Wisdom from the Dying by Julie Interrante (Compassionate Arts Publishing, 2009)

APPENDIX B

What makes a method (or non method) Buddhist is the fact that it promotes the final awakening that Buddha experienced—the awakening into the nature of consciousness as pure and unstructured. When we understand Buddhism in this way, two things become apparent. First, "Buddhism" exists outside of Buddhism, since many people have realized their real nature having never heard about the Buddha or Buddhism. Second—many of the teachings, methods, interactions and institutions that are called Buddhist are not Buddhist, because they don't awaken people to their ultimate, unconditioned nature. Instead, they condition people's experience or leave them with a set of beliefs.

—Peter Fenner

APPENDIX C

The "Aboriginal Dreamtime" is that part of aboriginal culture which explains the origins and culture of the land and its people. Aborigines have the longest continuous cultural history of any group of people on Earth—dating back—by some estimates—65,000 years. Dreamtime is Aboriginal Religion and Culture. The Dreamtime contains many parts: It is the story of things that have happened, how the universe came to be, how human beings were created and how the Creator intended for humans to function within the cosmos.

As with all other cultures—it speaks of Earth's Creation by Gods and Goddesses—some of whom were kind hearted—while others were cruel. The Australian Aborigines speak of *jiva* or *guruwari*, a *seed power* deposited in the earth. In the Aboriginal worldview, every meaningful activity, event, or life process that occurs at a particular place leaves behind a vibrational residue in the earth, as plants leave an image of themselves as seeds. The shape of the land—its mountains, rocks, riverbeds, and waterholes—and its unseen vibrations echo the events that brought that place into creation. Everything in the natural world is a symbolic footprint of the metaphysical beings whose actions created our world. As with a seed, the potency of an earthly location is wedded to the memory of its origin. The Aborigines called this potency the "Dreaming" of a place, and this Dreaming constitutes the sacredness of the earth

—Robert Lawlor, *Faces of the First Day: Awakening in the Aboriginal Dreamtime*

APPENDIX D

According to the Maori mind, the doubling of kore meant not simply "non-being" or "annihilating nothingness", though it includes this meaning, but it went beyond this. By means of a thoroughgoing negativity, the negation itself turns into the most positive activity. It is the negation of negation. "Te Korekore" is the infinite realm of the formless and undifferentiated. It is the realm not so much of "non-being" but rather of "potential being". It is the realm of Primal and Latent energy from which the stuff of the Universe proceeds and from which all things evolve.

APPENDIX E

A note from one of my editors:

I think you need to issue a "health warning" to women who think they want to meet Kali in their lives and start to know her better!! Seriously. I continue my own befriending of her in my life. It ain't easy or "nice" to lose one's self-image and face all those parts so deeply buried. She is not for the faint of heart!

APPENDIX F

"Presponding," Not Re-Sponding

New Views on Perception

We are pondering Dick Bierman's work on perception. This experimental physicist at the University of Amsterdam did experiments that show we apparently know things 1 to 2 seconds before we see them. This convincing work seems to support timeless or time-reversible aspects of observation. In other words, we seem to know events before the physical event signal is actually received by our retinas. Seattle physicist John Cramer's quantum theory explanation of observation Quantum Mind is that there are forward and backward movements in time. He speaks of a "quantum exchange" between observer and observed before observations take place. It seems to us as if Bierman's work may lend us experimental validation for Cramer's ideas. In other words, the roots of observation are time-free exchanges. He calls our ability to know things before we receive physical signals, *"presponding"* instead of responding.

—Arny Mindell

INDEX

A

"A Blessing for One Who Is Exhausted" (O'Donohue) 26, 181
Aborigines 270-1
absolute nothingness, *See i te korekore*
Adeola (childhood friend) 65-6
alchemy 128, 261-2
Alfred (neighbor) 113
allopathy 178, 192
Anderson, Cindy 59, 61
anguish 3, 94, 108, 119, 126, 128, 201, 207, 218, 259, 262
Aotearoa 189, 229

B

Baez, Joan 66, 78
Baraz, James 243
bardo 86
Battler, Helen 238
being 3, 29-30, 70, 72, 127, 174, 178, 188, 192, 202, 208, 226-7, 229-30, 259-60, 263, 271
Berthe (friend) 116, 118-19
Bierman, Dick 275
Bruce (brother) 41, 54, 65, 67, 71, 83, 106-7, 109, 132, 137
Buddhism 72, 269

C

Chadwick, Helen 252, 282
Charlie (brother) 41, 65, 75, 77, 79, 84, 86, 88, 107
Charlotte (mother's friend) 62
choleh 175
Civil Rights Movement 66
Claudia (childhood friend) 62

Colette (Sidonie-Gabrielle Colette) 54
My Mother's House 54
Concerto de Aranjuez (Rodrigo) 78
Conrad, Emilie 193
consciousness 50, 59, 236, 269
Cramer, John 274
"creation poem" 130
creativity 44, 46

D

Dayton, Tian 219
  Heartwounds: The Impact of Unresolved Trauma and Grief Upon Relationships 219
de Gast, Ilke 240
death 56, 68, 71-3, 87, 109, 112, 125, 129, 141, 202, 204, 263
Death Is a Gateway: Songs for the Sacred Passage 157
deathlessness 68, 154, 207, 263
despair 3, 126-8, 177, 201, 209, 227, 230, 259
DiBello, Maria 241
dreaming 175, 188, 191, 260, 271
dreamtime (Aboriginal) 270
Durrell, Gerald 54

My Family and Other Animals 54

E

England 106-7, 174, 179

F

father 41, 45-6, 48, 50, 54, 79, 93, 105, 133, 157, 200
  alcoholism 93-4
  full moon 154-6, 200, 202-3
  my portrait 53
  a thousand hands 47-8
Fenner, Peter 3, 269
Fincher (teacher) 64
forgiveness 86, 94
France 106-7, 109-10, 113, 125, 154, 174, 258
Frankel, Estelle 200, 268
  Sacred Therapy: Jewish Spiritual Teachings on Emotional Healing and Inner Wholeness 200, 268
Fromm, Erich 26, 65

G

Garriano, Mario 66
Goddi. *See* mother
grief 31, 108, 126, 128, 173
Grimm's Fairy Tales 54
guruwari 271

H

Hawai'i 219, 247
  Kipukamaluhia 21-2
Heartwounds: The Impact of Unresolved Trauma and Grief Upon Relationships (Dayton) 219
Hendrix, Christine 248
Hill, Barbara 235
Hundred Years' War 110

I

i te korekore 227
India 141, 151
Io 226

J

James, Henry 48
James, William 48
Jenny (Starr's daughter) 24-5, 28
jiva 271
Joanna (seminar participant) 225-9
Joyce, Tom 165

K

Kali (goddess) 151, 176
keening 108-9, 201
King, Martin Luther Jr. 66
koan 132, 189`
kore 272
Krishnamurti 106

Kübler-Ross, Elisabeth 109, 202
Kushi, Michio 127

L

Lawlor, Robert 271
letters 235-44, 246-9, 251-2
Lindner, Evelyn G. 251
Louis (Madame Alibert's son) 114-15
Lyme disease 173-4

M

Macy, Joanna 26, 187
Madame Alibert (neighbor) 113-15
Maori mourning tradition 126
Martin (husband) 107
Martin, Jennifer J. 239, 268
Massachusetts 105
Massell, Deborah 244-5
Mexico 24, 65, 75
Mindell, Arnold 175, 188, 224
miracle 3, 55-6, 65, 70, 76, 83, 94, 99, 152, 181
Monsieur Poujade (goat seller) 116
mother 41-4, 50, 57, 61, 85, 87, 95, 106, 132-3, 137, 141
  Charlie's death 84, 86, 93, 105, 218
  poems 129

protest march 66
summer art classes 57-8, 64-5, 67, 71
third of May 85, 132, 143
My Family and Other Animals (Durrell) 54
My Mother's House (Colette) 54

N

New Zealand, *see* Aotearoa
Nixon, Lucille 63, 69
non-being. *See* nothingness
Norkinu (horse) 61
nothingness 207, 209, 226, 272

O

O'Donohue, John 26, 181
  "A Blessing for One Who Is Exhausted" 181

P

perception 65, 74, 182, 213, 274
Plum Village 204, 249
Presponding 274-5
Puycalvel 110, 113, 125, 144

Q

Quan Yin 72, 176
quantum exchange 275
quantum theory 274

R

"Reason Is Powerless in the Expression of Love" (Rumi) 169
"Renascence" (St. Vincent Millay) 26, 68-9, 71, 261
Rodrigo, Joaquin 78
  Concerto de Aranjuez 78
Rumi, Jalal al-Din 166, 169, 192
  "Reason Is Powerless in the Expression of Love" 169
  "The Cure for Pain Is in the Pain" 192
  "This We Have Now" 129
Russell, Bertrand 48
Ryan, Michele 165, 168

S

Sacred Therapy: Jewish Spiritual Teachings on Emotional Healing and Inner Wholeness (Frankel) 200, 268
Santiago, Antonio 86-7
Satie, Erik 54
  Trois Gymnopédies 54
Sawatsky, Jarem 249-50
Shanti Nilaya 109
Shapiro, Vida 64
shibui 42, 45, 63, 112

"Song of No Coming and
    No Going" (Thich) 26,
    154, 203-4, 249
Soubira family 111, 119
St. Vincent Millay, Edna 68,
    261
  "Renascence" 26, 68-9, 71, 261
Starr, Mirabai 24, 27
suffering 4, 30-2, 68, 87, 94,
    101, 128, 152, 173, 201,
    235-6, 240, 251, 259, 263
Sufi 71, 166, 168, 252, 258
symptoms 94, 175, 177-8, 183,
    188, 191-2, 224, 226, 258
synesthesia 224

T

Tao (concept) 106
Tao (son) 109-11, 114, 120,
    132, 134, 137, 141
"The Cure for Pain Is in the
    Pain" (Rumi) 192
Thich Nhat Hahn 26, 154,
    203-4, 249
  "Song of No Coming and
    No Going" 203
"This We Have Now" (Rumi)
    129
Trois Gymnopédies (Satie) 54

U

"Unbroken, The" 4, 10, 163,
    167-8, 173, 200, 258, 267

V

Varda, Yanko 46
Vers River 133
von Bingen, Hildegard 212

W

"We Shall Overcome" 66
"Who Is in My Temple?"
    (unknown) 155
wishlessness 56, 69, 99, 119,
    260
wu wei 199

Z

Zen 43, 109, 112, 132

There is a brokenness
    out of which comes the unbroken,
a shatteredness out of which blooms the unshatterable.
There is a sorrow
    beyond all grief which leads to joy
and a fragility out of whose depths emerges strength.
There is a hollow space too vast for words
through which we pass with each loss,
out of whose darkness we are sanctioned into being.
There is a cry deeper than all sound
whose serrated edges cut the heart
    as we break open
to the place inside which is unbreakable
    and whole,
    while learning to sing.

Rashani

Raised throughout childhood to appreciate the perennial teachings at the core of all spiritual traditions, Rashani has recorded fifteen albums and created more than 350 collages in celebration of the diversity of world wisdom. She spent twenty-two years in Europe, during which time she renovated a 17th century stone farmhouse with her son in the south of France. Since 1991 Rashani has lived simply and sustainably on the Big Island of Hawai'i where she offers individual and group retreats several times a year. A designer, builder, tree planter and landscape artist, she has created two sanctuaries with the help of many retreatants and friends, in the remote district of Ka'ū. She also offers retreats, satsangs, sessions and concerts throughout the world. For further information, visit:

www.rashani.com

All artwork and poetry is by Rashani Réa,
unless otherwise specified.

Jacket design and photograph of Rashani
by Matthew Tao Giuffrida

Photograph of irises by Sonja Trier

Three recordings of "The Unbroken" are available:

Helen Chadwick, who composed a choral version,
can be reached at www.helenchadwick.com

Justin Weaver, who composed a work for soprano,
Tamara Bevard, and piano, can be reached at
improvist@usa.net

A spoken version by Rashani is also available,
as are signed prints, cards, and information
about retreats in Hawai'i, at www.rashani.com

Lightning Source UK Ltd.
Milton Keynes UK
UKHW011818010419
340294UK00001B/45/P